SCARED SPEECHLESS

My Crazy Journey to Mastering Fear

ROY ROSELL

Scared Speechless – My Crazy Journey to Mastering Fear
by Roy Rosell

For permission to make copies of any part of this work, please submit your request to:

Roy Rosell
P.O. Box 383, Alhambra CA, 91802
Or, email Roy at royscaredspeechless@gmail.com

Website: www.RoyRosell.com

Cover design by: Jim Paniagua
Edited by: Michael K. Ireland

This material is offered for entertainment purposes only. The author of this book does not dispense medical or psychological advice, or prescribe the use of any technique as a form of treatment for physical, emotional, or medical issues without the advice of a physician, either directly or indirectly. No professional or mentorship advice is intended. The intent of the author is only to offer information of a general and entertaining nature to help you in your quest for achieving emotional well-being. In the event you use any of the information in this book for yourself, which is your constitutional right, the author assumes no responsibility for your actions. Please consult your physician or mental health provider if you are in need of health-related assistance on a physical or mental level, and your spiritual adviser if you require spiritual guidance. The author accepts no responsibility and is not liable in any way for your reliance upon or your use of the information contained in this book. Thank you. Rock on.

I have tried to recreate events, locales and conversations from my memories of them. In order to maintain their anonymity in some instances, I have changed the names of individuals and I may have changed some identifying characteristics and details such as physical properties, occupations and places of residence.

Printed in the United States of America

First Printing, 2018

ISBN: 978-0-692-98441-3
LCCN: 2017919308

For my parents. I'm eternally grateful for the tough, but unconditional love.
And to fear and doubt: You almost convinced me I couldn't do this.
What now?!

Contents

Acknowledgments

I would like to express my sincere gratitude to everyone who has helped me in this seemingly endless journey to finish *Scared Speechless*. Thanks, Dad, for the bi-weekly, "Am I going to see this book published in my lifetime, or are you waiting until I'm six feet under?" to get me back on track. Thanks, Mom, for always telling me "You are the BEST writer en el mundo, hijo!" to keep me motivated. Thanks too to my mentor, Dermot McQuarrie, for his wisdom, guidance, and hilarity throughout the process. To Bryce Hubner, for the invaluable feedback on the abysmal first versions of my manuscript, my undying gratitude. And to Jim Paniagua, master designer, thank you for your time, effort, and friendship, and for making the book cover a reality.

Finally, to those who doubted me at every stage of my life: thanks for the boost.

Introduction

"Hi, my name is _____ and I saw your video on YouTube.
I felt _____ (a- inspired; b- confused; c- pissed-off) by
your speech and decided to message you for help. I have
been struggling with the fear of public speaking for ___
years, and it makes my body ____ [adjective or verb], my
face ____ [adjective or verb] and my confidence go to
____ [expletive noun]. I know that if this stays the same,
I'm going to: a- Drop out of_____ [school name]; b-
Continue doing _____ [low-paying occupation] making
$___ [single digit number] an hour for the rest of my
____ [expletive] life; c- [Insert other miserable outcome
in descriptive sentence]. Please tell me how you learned
to manage your fear, you lucky _____ [noun]!"

This is the basic template of the hundreds of emails and messages
I've received from people trying to control their fear. But about
a week before starting *Scared Speechless*, I received an email that
left me thunderstruck:

"Hello Roy, I've been struggling with the fear of public speaking since I was fifteen. I'm afraid to introduce myself to the class, or to answer a question that requires more than two words—even if I know the answer. Presentations are my ultimate fear—I prefer to receive an F than do a five-minute presentation. It's a monster that never goes away. Do you know what makes me most sad about it? I wasn't like this at all before the age of fifteen. My dream was to become a news reporter. I'm thirty-four today. I'm happy for you, my friend, but this monster is holding me tight. This has destroyed me."

*Holy crap…*I thought. Minus wanting to be a news reporter, this is a letter I would have written had I not learned to control my fear. Just as it was for the reader who sent that email, my fear of public speaking was a monster that dragged my self-esteem on a leash everywhere it went. I couldn't shake it off for the life of me.

What I wish I'd known when I started my battle is that fear is not an incurable disease. Fear is just a glass barrier waiting to be shattered and, once shattered, there's nothing that can hold you back. But before I get into too much detail about all of that, allow me to introduce myself.

I'm Roy Rosell, son of Hebe Rosell and Roy Rosell Sr. (you'll soon meet them and their 'Spanglish' wisdom). I'm half-Argentinian, half-Peruvian, so that means I have a Ron-Swanson-esque obsession with food, I have broken at least twenty bones playing *futbol*, I enjoy (but am terrible at)

Introduction

Latin dancing, and I'm more "touchy-feely" than most people. The touchiness has led to some painfully awkward social interactions:

Guy:	"Hi, I'm Mark. It's a pleasure to meet you."
Me:	"The pleasure is mine, Mark!"
	I move in for the customary Latino kiss on the cheek
Mark:	"I didn't mean to lead you on…."

Aside from being a food-obsessed, soccer-loving, two-left-footed, touchy Argentinian/Peruvian, who I am today is thanks to the struggles of my past. Between the ages of ten and twenty-three, I suffered from a terrorizing fear of public speaking. I don't mean the "...giving speeches makes my voice quiver," or the "I get so nervous, public speaking is hard!" type of public speaking fear. I mean the "I haven't slept for two nights; I just spent thirty minutes crying; crouched over a toilet bowl with nerve-induced nausea; and I ended up skipping my presentation—but I'd probably have passed out on stage anyway" type of public speaking fear. I've ditched important classes, job interviews, and some potentially life-changing opportunities to avoid standing up in front of an audience.

The process of figuring out how to overcome my fear was…crazy. Frantic. Absurd. Yet, sometimes, it was entirely logical. It took me twelve years to figure out—finally—how to defeat the curse that was eating away my potential (and my sanity).

Becoming the lover of public speaking I am today hasn't been easy. Whereas before I'd be more inclined to claw my eyes out than speak in front of a group, now, I look for every opportunity to rock the socks off an audience. Here's a list of the highlights of my journey so far. I:

3

- have been a lover of public speaking (ages four to ten, and age twenty-three to present).

- have been terrified of public speaking (age ten to twenty-three).

- have suffered from social anxiety, due to my crippling fear of public speaking (age ten to nineteen).

- have had an enormous afro hair-style, that ranged in size from four to twelve inches off my head, in all directions (ages thirteen to twenty-six).

- have sometimes been a loner, especially during my entire first year of high school (age fourteen). That year, I frequently walked across campus pretending to text friends on my phone, and spent lunch breaks sad and alone in desolate hallways.

- played in a punk rock band (age fifteen to sixteen), made new friends my parents didn't approve of, and started wearing all black—partly to fit in and partly to conceal my public speaking nerve-induced sweat.

- have participated in a campus-wide "Say-What" Karaoke competition—thereby making an absolute fool of myself in front of the entire student/faculty population. But I had an awesome time and was infused with the hope that maybe I could overcome my fear (age seventeen).

- graduated from high school with a dreadful GPA, leaving my education-obsessed parents miserably disappointed (and, I suspect, seriously considering disowning me (age seventeen)).

- started university at Cal Poly Pomona with high hopes, good intentions, and a crippling fear of public speaking.

- joined another punk rock band in hopes that it would help me overcome my fear of being on stage. Toured most of the Western U.S. (age eighteen to twenty-one).

- had eight internships during college in the sports and entertainment industries (age nineteen to twenty-three), including one notable internship at NBCUniversal where I had the chance to solidify my entertainment industry career path for good.

- moved to London, England for a few months (helloooo lifelong debt!) to work and play for a lower division soccer team, Sutton United (soccer fanatics may have heard of their FA Cup heroics) (age twenty-one).

- graduated as the President's Scholar at Cal Poly Pomona and gave the commencement speech to 15,000 people (age twenty-three).

- overcame my fear of public speaking, and learned to love the stage again (age twenty-three).

- worked in music licensing/marketing at Fox Sports; in content marketing at the American Youth Soccer Organization; in product marketing for a now defunct tech company that built apps for Major League Baseball and Liverpool Football Club. Now, I'm managing marketing at a cryptocurrency consulting firm out of Beverly Hills (age twenty-three to present).

I'll dive into a lot of the scenarios mentioned above throughout my book, but the focus is on the second bullet point: the twelve-plus years—from fifth grade to the end of college—when I lived with a horrifying fear of public speaking. I'll tell you how, in just three short months, I found my way back to the first bullet point: loving public speaking.

That said, there are a few things I want to warn you about this book, in hopes of making your reading experience highly gratifying—and less roller-coaster-ish. When I started writing *Scared Speechless*, I had a meticulously-crafted outline that I had every intention of following. And that's what I did, everything was going swimmingly. But a few chapters in, a feeling of dissatisfaction began to consume me. With every chapter I completed, my disappointment intensified. I stopped enjoying the process. About fifty pages in, I stopped writing.

It's always been a dream of mine to write a book, I thought. *Why the hell am I not enjoying it?*

I couldn't pinpoint the problem. The writing was organized—I had one story per chapter that perfectly supported each lesson, and I'd concluded each chapter with an entertaining summary. *Scared Speechless* was on its way to becoming everything I wanted it to be. After much deliberation and soul-searching, I finally figured out what was going on.

What I realized was that while my outline was keeping me organized, it was also a destructive force—like a steamroller, it was crushing my passion and ripping the life out of my narrative. It was forcing me to tell my story in a logical progression, as if the lessons unfolded in succession, one-tidy-learning-curve-after-the-other. In reality, the journey was a nauseating, soul-crushing, deliriously electrifying, down-in-the-ditch depressing, bountifully rewarding, nerve-shredding ride. Sure, eventually I got my floundering ducks in a row and figured out an action plan to control my fear. But my twelve-year struggle with the fear of public speaking didn't follow an organized, templatized, rational sequence.

So, I tossed the idea that "I should" create an eloquent, well-structured book. I shredded my outline, tossed out the first fifty pages—and started typing. You hold in your hands (or see on your digital reader) what I ended up with. It's a bit wild—the words come in equal parts from my heart and from my brain. That's the good news. The bad news is that the decision to dump the outline turned what might have been a year-long process into a five-year, all-encompassing project. The book morphed, evolved, and ultimately, settled into its current form.

I'm telling you all of this because due to this free-form, ripped-from-my-heart approach, I time-travel in this book—a lot. I might start a chapter in the first person, as current-day, calm, collected, confident Roy; then suddenly jump back in time to speak to you as my weird, wired fifteen-year-old-punk-rock self; then lurch forward to my lost and lonely twenty-year-old self; only to bounce right back to present day a couple sentences later. And you might be thinking: "What. The. Hell. Roy?" All the jumping about might make you feel, well, a bit disoriented. Sometimes, I'll revisit a point I made earlier in the book, fifteen chapters later, from a different angle. And again, you might be thinking: "Roy, you spaz. We've heard this already. Onto something new!" But stick with me, okay? It's like when you get sucked into the event horizon of a black hole—things are a bit discombobulated. But once you get blasted out the other side—you're in a new reality, you're no longer mystified—and everything makes sense. As you'll see (once you get used to my time-travellin' rhythm), many of the themes I cover in the book were so critical in my struggle that by necessity, they come up time and time again. I couldn't stay planted in the present or bring you along on a linear path, the true story simply didn't unfold that way. So, we twist, we turn, we zig and we zag—but I promise you, we get where we're going and the circuitous route will be well worth the journey.

Also, you'll notice that I talk about "my struggle," "my battle," "my journey," "my fight," etc.—a lot. These terms are used in reference to my war with glossophobia (the fear of public speaking), which as I noted began in fifth grade and continued until the end of college. It was then, right at the end of my college days, that I implemented my action plan and learned to love public speaking again.

So, when I talk about "those months" or "those three months," I'm referring to the three months leading up to my university commencement speech, in which I crafted and acted on an ingenious "Plan" I'd developed to overcome my fear. The resulting speech (I nailed it!) marked the end of "my journey" and the end of Fear's control over me.

Fear, Doubt, Failure

I talk about three major themes in this book: fear, doubt, and failure. Each played a critical role in my journey towards loving public speaking, and I wouldn't be being genuine if I just covered the story of my victory over each of these obstacles in a chapter. These challenges were pervasive, all-consuming, and each was with me all the way. So, you'll see them mentioned throughout the book, and in some places, I'll dive in—real deep—to reveal the impact they had on me—both on my trials and my triumphs.

I wanted this book to be as real, as authentic, and as organic as possible. Glossophobia is an issue that many of us don't know how to overcome, and most of the time, it requires much more than just following a step-by-step, how-to guide. Before you build your action plan to tackle your fear, a mental shift is required. And to experience that mental shift, there are things you must realize—and some of these things are more vital than others. In my opinion, the important things are worth repeating. So—you guessed it—I repeat them.

My story won't reveal "Five Surefire Ways to Make Millions from Public Speaking" or "The Ultimate Secret to Eliminating Fear in Three Easy Steps." In this age of quantum information, there are no secrets. But if you're fighting to overcome your fear like I did, I know what you're going through. I have felt the dark sensation of hopelessness you're feeling right now.

"But," you might be thinking, "why should I listen to you, Roy? The only things I know about you are that you don't like outlines and you repeat yourself a lot."

That's a solid question. Why? Because whereas many authors of books on this subject might struggle to fit their achievements onto a mile-long scroll; I'd need a twenty-series anthology to record all my botched presentations, embarrassing moments, and scared speechless screw-ups. I've been to the deepest depths of public speaking hell, suffered the agony of uncontrollable pre-presentation anxiety too many times to count, and stood motionless, mute, mumbling, in front of countless audiences. And after twelve years of this, I emerged from that hell, unscathed, and ready to take on any podium and speak in front of any audience. So, what's in it for you? Well, because I screwed up so much along the way, what took me twelve years should have taken me no more than three months. If I could go back in time with the knowledge I have now, I'd have avoided all this pain and gotten over my fear far more quickly. But I can't, so I'll just share with you what I've learned, so you can implement it yourself (and even if you're just reading for entertainment, you'll still enjoy it).

If you're looking for advice on becoming a famous public speaker and traveling the world making millions on a speaking circuit, shoot me an email in a couple of years and I might have a strategy for you. But right now, my hope is that my story will inspire you to have the courage to defeat the fears that have been holding your amazing potential hostage.

"Ha!" you're thinking. "If I had a nickel for every time…."

I get it. You'd be rolling around in a mound of nickels. The thing is, I'd be right there next to you, body-boarding down that colossal collection of coinage.

When I was riddled with fear, I was an average guy with flaws and insecurities, on a tireless journey to discover success and bliss. Today, I'm still that average guy, with far-fetched aspirations and unrealized dreams. But the thing is, I'm not crippled by fear anymore. I've learned to use fear to my advantage: to motivate me and push me to heights I never believed attainable. Now, my potential is limitless. After years of saying, "I've tried everything, I'll never get over it," I worked hard, and maintained laser focus. After three months of concentrated determination, I vanquished fear. The best part is, it wasn't nearly as difficult as I'd imagined.

You're probably thinking, "Roy, there's like five billion resources to help me overcome my fear of public speaking. Why you? Why your book?" You're right. After all, a Google, Bing or _____ (enter less popular search engine here, you rebel) search will reveal thousands of public speaking guide books, motivational seminars, therapy centers specializing in fears, and step-by-step guides to target this problem.

I've read half of those books, felt the resulting surge of motivation, then watched it fade to oblivion at the first glimpse of a podium. I've been to therapy. It didn't fix me. I've watched videos with promises of a better life, felt stirred to action, then froze in my tracks when things got hard. It wasn't them, it was me. For me, it was never a matter of "finding the secret" or the perfect "how-to list" to kill my fear. It was about adopting a completely new state of mind—one primed to weaken fear, doubt, hesitation, and all of the limiting mindsets that held me back. It took me twelve years to adopt that mindset. I want to save you that time. That is why you should read my book.

I hope you enjoy *Scared Speechless*, and I hope my journey from fear to freedom will help to ease your path forward. So, read the book, do the exercises, and then get out there and wow 'em!

PART I

MY LIFE WITH GLOSSOPHOBIA

CHAPTER 1:

The Speech

"To live a life of excellence, you will have to take risks. You will have to step into new territory and climb new mountains. If you're up to something that's as big as you are, it's going to be scary. If it feels perfectly safe, you are probably underachieving. To leave your mark in the world, you will have to stand someplace you've never been willing to stand before. And you will have to have the courage to aspire to excellence."

— DEBBIE FORD

June 15, 2013
Cal Poly Pomona – Commencement Ceremony

I sat on stage, looking out into the sunny quad of black gowns, proud parents, and the aloof expressions of students who couldn't care less. Some were graduates a lot smarter than me. Some likely felt they should be giving this speech. Others probably thought, "This funky-haired fool is the President's Scholar?" And then, there were my friends and family, all of whom expected one hell of a show.

It was the day I had been preparing for my entire life. About an hour into the ceremony, the words that signaled my introduction drifted towards me in slow motion. "There's another student the College would like to recognize, the recipient of the President's honor."

Wow…this is it. God help me….

It was the 2013 College of Business commencement ceremony at Cal Poly Pomona. I had been selected as the President's Scholar by the university's elected officials, and the "honor" of presenting at the ceremony had been bestowed upon me. The Dean would introduce me for another minute or so; I'd stride boldly to the microphone; stare out into the crowd of 15,000 grads—some eager, some emotional, some staring blankly at the grass—and conduct a speech. It was the speech that I had never, not even in my wildest dreams, imagined I'd be capable of, the presentation that, after twelve years of despair, tears, and trashed opportunities, would end either in glorious victory or in utter disgrace. Everything I have ever lost, failed at, or suffered endlessly for culminated in this moment.

A recurring nightmare I'd had for most of my life was of me standing in front of a large audience, opening my mouth, and vocalizing a barely audible squeak. My reaction to this nightmare was the same as my response to dreams where waves of spiders tried to kill me: I'd drop to the floor, assume a fetal position, shut my eyes, and pray for the dream to end. People say that dreams come true for those who work hard—I wasn't aware the same applied for nightmares.

But this time, the price of cowering was steep, and the crowd was larger than the paltry 5,000 I'd dreamed of. As the Dean droned on, my mind began to race. I recalled how I'd died inside with each nonsensical word I'd muttered in front of classes of twenty students; I remembered the sleepless nights before presentations when I'd spent seven hours staring up at my bedroom ceiling, an intense pressure in my stomach, contemplating the terrors that awaited me in the morning; I replayed my countless botched presentations and the suffering I'd endured—all of this just seconds before the most important speech of my life.

I thought of the award the university's President was about to present to me. Did I deserve it? Probably not. All through school I'd been plagued with a pitiable inability to speak in front of an audience, often ditching classes on speech days to avoid the gut-wrenching humiliation. How could I deserve it?

"Ladies and Gentlemen, Mr. Roy Rosell," the Dean said. We shook hands. He presented me with the President's Scholar award. I stared down at it—part of me felt like crying with joy. The other part of me thought, *what the hell did I get myself in to?* The Dean stepped back. He looked at me, nodded, and gestured towards the dais, as if to say, "Take it away, Roy." He returned to his seat.

The crowd fell silent. The sound of my heartbeat broke through the hush and pounded in my ears, sending tremors through my body. My breath quickened. I stepped forward. I saw my family, front row, on the edge of their seats, anticipating my first word. As I moved toward it, the podium seemed to recede into the distance, floating outward, above the sea of unfamiliar faces. A drop of sweat materialized on the back of my neck. Another step—two—three. My footsteps sounded hollow on the platform. I felt wobbly, light-headed. I reached out to steady myself on the stand. I couldn't feel my left leg. I placed the folder containing my speech on the microphone stand. I looked up, breathed in, opened my mouth to speak.

Nothing. Nada. The words didn't come. I turned quickly away—the silence seemed eternal. My heartbeat doubled, my body temperature rose, every clever tactic I had planned abandoned me. I took a deep breath, turned towards the crowd, and spoke.

"I had to cut my hair to fit this cap on, but it's still not working."

The words emerged as if from a pot of molasses. My attempt at breaking the ice fell flat—there was scattered laughter, but none of it seemed sincere. *Awkward.*

Another bead of sweat formed, at the corner of my temple.

Was I about to crash and burn in front of 15,000 people?

Hovering over the podium, I looked down at my speech. Then, I remembered something else that could have made me feel panicked, like a crippled cat trying to bury a turd in a frozen pond: It wasn't the script the Dean had approved. In fact, it was the version the university's top officials had deemed wholly unsuitable for the proceedings and had asked me to rewrite. As I'd waited to be summoned to the podium, I had sneakily replaced the approved speech with the rejected speech. I was about to present it to 15,000 people—might as well talk about something I felt passionate about, right?

But during this all-too-familiar situation, completely vulnerable in front of an audience, in a predicament with a high probability of disaster, something was missing. Dread. Panic. Fear. For the first time in twelve years, I wasn't overcome with crippling terror. Had I botched a joke at the beginning of a speech a few months earlier, the rest of that presentation would have been me doing everything I could to refrain from crumbling. But this time, as much as my mind, body, and experience told me I should be suffering an internal meltdown, I remained composed.

After that first joke, the magnitude of the situation hit me. I felt nervous—really nervous. But as I looked across the vast expanse of black gowns and high expectations, I was smacked in the face with an unmistakable aura of opportunity. My hands shivered, my palms were drenched in sweat, but I couldn't wait to tell my story.

I faced the microphone and gave the speech of a lifetime.

"…God bless you all," I said at the end of my speech, "And thank you for this wonderful opportunity."

Holy crap, I did it.

I exhaled, and looked out at the audience as they erupted in applause and cheers. My family rose to their feet, as did many others in the audience. I was shocked. As I faced the audience, basking in the glory of their appreciation, my throat started to quiver, and tears flooded my eyes. As treacly as it sounds, this was a lifelong dream come true. Just three months before the commencement speech, I would've probably considered amputating my right arm if it meant not having to stand on a stage in front of that many people. But there I was, I had faced the thing that had terrorized me for twelve years.

I was on top of the world.

CHAPTER 2:

Nosedive Into Public Speaking Hell

"Roycito, por qué you so nervous, you are so guapo and esmart!"

— Mom

For the twelve years preceding that presentation, I had dreamt about moments just like it, only to awaken to the depressing reality that I couldn't even conduct a speech to a class of fifteen without dying inside. If someone had told me at any point during my time in college that I'd be giving the speech at my graduation ceremony, I would have laughed dismissively, gone home, then spent all night considering dropping out of college in case it was true. I wish I were joking, but my fear was that destructive.

Before glossophobia took control of my life, I loved giving speeches. Hearing the hysterical laughter, the gasps of astonishment and hums of approval following something I'd said brought a feeling of joy that couldn't be replicated. On stage, I felt happy, admired, appreciated—even important. Off stage, I couldn't wait for my next presentation. Standing in front of an audience was my favorite place to be.

Sadly, that euphoria wouldn't last. My love for public speaking died in the fifth grade, beaten to a pulp by an invader named Fear. On that fateful day, the happy, carefree Roy perished, and the chronically stressed, anxious, risk-averse Roy was born.

The Onset of Glossophobia

McKinley Elementary School – Fifth Grade

It was the first of several presentation assignments of the school year at McKinley Elementary. I trembled with anticipation. When it was my turn to present, I walked confidently to the front of the classroom, looked at my friends, and flashed a smirk that said, "You ready for this?" I scanned the room, let out a long, exaggerated yawn, then unleashed my first joke: "I'm so sorry everyone; I'm very sleepy. People who say they sleep like a baby must not have one!" It was a joke I had used a few times before and each time, it had had teachers gasping for air and students laughing their heads off.

Cackling laughter erupted from the back corner of the room where my two buddies were sitting. No one else made a peep, so their uproar quickly faded to silence. I was confused—*did I say it wrong? Was I not loud enough?* No, it wasn't that—I'd had jokes fall flat before, but this one went…splat.

I imagined what my classmates were thinking: *What a dweeb!* I stopped the negative thoughts from taking control of my mind, and carried on. I did my best to ignore the growing pressure in my midsection, the stream of sweat flowing down my back, and the tremor in my voice, which became more noticeable with each word I squeezed out of my rapidly contracting trachea.

About thirty seconds later, I fired full force with what I thought was going to be the greatest joke in McKinley history: "By the way, it's so cold outside that I saw Javier (the school's wannabe gangster) pull his pants up! I could barely see his butt this time!"

Javier was a total bully, so I was convinced that poking fun at the most menacing kid in school would be a hit, so I cracked up. But after a few seconds, my laughter withered. Aside from some nervous snorts from my friends' corner, the room was silent. Not even a pity chuckle. I looked to my friends for support, but all I saw was concern. They'd never seen me fail this hard.

My hands trembled, my voice shook, and the pressure in the pit of my stomach intensified. *How could they do this to me?* I looked at the audience, as I had so many times before in years past, but this time, I wasn't smiling. And for the first time ever, neither were they.

My eyes darted downwards, looking frantically for a speck on the ground, a floating piece of lint—anything. One hand went into my pocket, came out of my pocket, I scratched my leg, itched my ear, picked at my eye, then my hand went back into my pocket. The other hand wiped forehead sweat onto my shorts. My right knee began to rub against the desk in front of me. That desk had been an annoyance, a gulf between me and my friends, but now it became a shield—a protector between me and the demons I faced.

I had never felt this terror or this pressure in my stomach. In desperation, I skipped entire sections of my presentation and talked at double-speed. I had presented to the kids in my class many times and

I knew how to recover from an unsuccessful joke—I had confidence in my ability to entertain. Now, the familiar faces sitting in front of me were intimidating. I was falling into that abyss; there was nothing left in my survival kit to save me.

As I reached the conclusion of my presentation, I heard a rising chorus of whispers and restrained snickers coming from the left side of the room. Within seconds, it intensified into a symphony of raucous laughter. *Finally!* I thought. *They're laughing! I knew I'd get them!* I looked up, smiling, proud, relieved to have finally made this hard-to-please audience chuckle. But they weren't laughing at my jokes.

"Gross!" a student in the middle of the room howled, covering his mouth in pretend shock. "Eww!" hissed another kid sitting in the second row, struggling to contain his glee. Everyone was staring at my chest—pointing, laughing, concealing their mouths behind their hands in disbelief. They'd laughed because I was overweight. More specifically, they'd laughed because I had man-boobs—or, as my friends called them, *moobs*.

I tried to keep my head down, finish my speech, and get the hell off that stage. I was crippled with terror, frozen in place at the front of the classroom. My face went numb, I was overcome with sadness—the kind of lingering dread that accompanies heartbreak or death. My lips trembled, my eyes flooded with tears. I fought as hard as I could to salvage my crumbling social image. I felt myself falling apart. Seconds later, eleven-year-old Roy burst into tears in front of all his classmates.

Before that moment, I'd never seen public speaking as being any different than talking soccer with my buddies at recess. I sashayed around school with my head held high, no concern for the moob-peaks bulging

24

from my chest. On speech days, I waltzed onto stage and confidently conducted fun presentations that had even the sternest teachers cracking a smile. Before that day, I was exactly the version of myself that I spent the next twelve years trying to revive.

After the moobs debacle, I saw the stage differently. It became a place of judgement, where my deepest insecurities came to light, where every word I spoke and every move I made was scrutinized. Gone was my comfort at the podium—now, it was a punishing platform, its blinding spotlight exposing my every fault and insecurity. It made me feel unsafe.

For many people, the genesis of public speaking fear begins with an onstage incident: forgetting lines, boring the audience to death, having a technical malfunction and standing awkwardly onstage for what feels like eternity. For others, it's simply the start of social consciousness—the battle to be cool and to create a favorable persona.

To fight your own demons, it's important to understand how, when and why they began to dominate your world.

Exercise #1: Know thyself, know your fears

Note: For the exercises and "Risk This" challenges in this book, it's important that you write down your answers to the listed questions. So, find yourself a nice notebook or journal before you get started!

You can't get rid of your fear until you know what it is you fear. So, ask yourself the following questions and write down your answers:

- Describe the event or situation that triggered your fear of public speaking. If there isn't one, describe what you think caused the onset of your fear.
- What aspect of public speaking do you fear the most?
- What do you think is stopping you from reducing your fear to a level you're comfortable with?

CHAPTER 3:
A Fear-Riddled Life

"All of us are born with a set of instinctive fears, of falling, of the dark, of lobsters, of falling on lobsters in the dark, or speaking before the Rotary Club, or the words 'some assembly required.'"

— DAVE BARRY

About a year after the onset of my glossophobia, in sixth grade, I wrote a letter to my future self, locked it up in a metal box, and buried it in the back yard. I threw the key in my neighbor's tree. When miraculously I found the box at the beginning of my final year in college, and plucked off the rusty lock, I expected a glimpse into my boyhood crushes, a passionate account of my soccer dreams, or something about James M. Salamander, a character I'd created and often wrote absurd stories about throughout my childhood. Instead, in big block letters, I read:

Dear Dummy,

I don't know how old you are now, but I hope you are not scared like me of talking in class. If you are still scared, you are so lazy and a big dummy. Today, I almost cried talking because my voice was shaking so much and I sounded like such a motor mouse. Agghhhhhhhhhhh!! I want to like presentations again! I hope you do everything you can so you can be good at it. Don't be scared to try your best, because hey if you mess up, at least that's better than being too wimpy to try, like me :) . Also, try make people laugh and make them happy. I don't even try anymore because I'm too scared.... I wish I was like when I was a little kid, happy and cool. I don't know how to do that so you have to do it!

When I read the letter, a couple of things concerned me. Firstly, I thought, what the hell is a "motor mouse?" I suspected it was my younger self trying to say he sounded like a "motor mouth," or perhaps a "motor home," but I'm not sure if either of those make much sense. Secondly, couldn't he have brought this up with a counselor or with our parents? He had to send an insult-ridden plea to his future self? Lastly, *take it easy, past self—no need to be a jerk!*

But reading it also caused me to feel a wave of disappointment. I had failed to achieve what my younger self had asked of me. I had read over 100 books and 1,000 articles on public speaking since writing that letter, had gotten advice from public speaking experts, had plenty of resources within my reach to get better, and had spent eleven years trying to 'crack the code'…but still I spent my days hoping, wishing, and dreaming that one day, I would not dread giving speeches.

I asked myself: *Why am I still terrified of public speaking?* After all, it had been a decade since an audience had taunted my moobs or trashed my words. People weren't making fun of the way I looked or ridiculing the things I said anymore. *Why must I experience this panic-inducing horror about speaking in front of a class? Why does this feel impossible to overcome?*

It wasn't easy for me to figure out the answers to these questions. But through ego-crushing failures, soul-shattering screw-ups, and some epic successes on my journey to captivate an audience, I eventually did find the answers (and I'll reveal them in this book).

Throughout my seemingly hopeless journey, I felt as if it didn't matter how much I practiced, breathed, relaxed, studied, or worked on my confidence—I was doomed to a pathetic existence of crumbling at the sight of a lectern. I've felt hopeless and useless and have envisioned a future devoid of success in love, life, and career. I've been on the verge of quitting jobs and dropping out of school, I've lain awake on countless nights, plagued with dread. I've been mocked, I've felt mortified. I've wished I could hit *reset*, be reborn with a different name, in a different place, with none of the traits that defined who I was—Roy, the glossophobe.

I didn't choose to feel this way—I didn't stumble upon glossophobia, accidentally consume it, or smoke it in a pipe. I could probably have been a better friend, a better son, more of a humanitarian—but there's no way I did anything to warrant this punishment. No one deserves this hell.

I often wondered: *What happened to cool Roy?* The Roy who brought a roomful of second graders to their feet following a sincere speech about the epic-ness of crayons? The Roy that charismatically performed an ABC's song-and-dance routine to a packed auditorium? That Roy had had everything under control back then. All the teachers had wished that Roy was their kid. I wanted to be him again, to be cool again.

Before kicking glossophobia's ass, I struggled, shirked, and suffered the emotional, physical, and social nightmare that is glossophobia for the span of time between fifth grade and the end of college—all the while putting on a big, fake smile, pretending—"Everything's fine!"

But about a year after opening the embittered letter from the younger me, I accomplished my mission. I felt like my former self on stage again. Finally. People stopped falling asleep during my talks, side conversations halted. Texting during my presentations became almost non-existent. My audiences were focused, happy, they laughed at my jokes, asked intriguing questions. Best of all, in off-situations when my audience wasn't spellbound, it didn't affect me the way it used to. I just tried a little harder.

But before that happened, I was a mess.

A Sweaty, Pale, Trembling Mess

Two months before starting college

One day in the summer leading to my freshman year of college, I picked up *The Quick and Easy Way to Effective Speaking* by Dale Carnegie. I read it three times. I wrote notes after every paragraph, drew arrows pointing to key ideas, and underlined the motivational portions. Eventually, it looked like I had handwritten the book and Dale had typed up notes on what I'd had to say.

Dale made everything sound obvious—as if getting over the fear of public speaking was like learning to tie a shoe—it just takes a positive attitude, repetition, and dedication. I felt pretty stupid for not being able to figure it out on my own. After desecrating the guide with scribbles and scrawls, I figured it wasn't the only public speaking book on the market. So, before implementing Dale's hallowed lessons, I made my way to the last bookstore within a fifteen-mile radius of my home for a shopping spree. I picked up *How to Develop Self-Confidence & Influence People by Public Speaking* and *Public Speaking for Success*, both by Dale Carnegie; Elmer Wheeler's *How I Mastered My Fear of Public Speaking; On Speaking Well*, by ex-presidential speechwriter Peggy Noonan; and an audio book titled *Speak to Win*, by a guy who looked scholarly.

I caught Mom on the computer searching, "I think my hijo has eschizophrenia, he is acting bery weird, I am bery worry for his mental health" (Mom hadn't mastered the art of the search engine yet)—but it didn't bother me. Detective Roy was onto something—reading those books gave me a boost of confidence, enough to see the sliver of light high above the ditch I was drowning in. I was still scared out of my mind of public speaking, but I was building a raft I could sail downstream on.

That summer, I must have read twenty books. And I'm a *really* slow reader, so that took up most of my days. With each book I finished and each lesson I implemented to sharpen my skillset, I noticed a slight improvement in my presentation prowess. I'd still twitch and tremble on stage, but it was more a shake than a quake.

My newfound obsession with reading public speaking self-help books sent my social life tumbling down into the aforementioned ditch. But reading wasn't the only thing affecting my social life. Due to my terrorizing fear of public speaking, I had to deal with:

Full Body Perspiration

Upon realizing I had an impending speech, my sweat glands freaked, and any chair I sat on would be marinated for the poor soul who had the misfortune of sitting on it next. It became my calling card—friends would point at puddles on benches and quip, "Roy! I see you took a break from working the corner last night!"

Dad bought me a "highly effective, dermatologist-recommended" aluminum chloride deodorant to disguise the armpit stains, but all it took was a teacher saying, "This semester, you'll be giving two presentations…" for the ditch water to start oozing through. I started wearing black clothing to help cover the stains. Mom was convinced it was a bad idea: "Ayyyyy Roycito, estas invitando a los demonios (you're inviting the demons)! Por favor, do not wear el negro so much!" I'd walk around shamefully, with toilet paper tucked into my armpits—no one had a clue. But the anxiety didn't go away.

Vampire-like Paleness

I was a vampiric shade of pale as it was; but once I knew I'd have to give a speech, I would morph from a run-of-the-mill, sun-deprived white kid to the spawn of Kristen Stewart and Frosty the Snowman. Being pale mortified me, especially when I was nervous. As a result, Mom would lecture endlessly in her catastrophe-littered Spanglish. "Roycito!" she would plead. "Por favor no go in the sun too much time! You are too blanco! Tu prima, she got el skeen problema por qué she too much en el sun. You have to put el sun lotion hijo! Ay, Dios mio!"

I was possessed by demonic spirits already; now I had el skeen problema to worry about as well? I decided wearing black was worth the life-threatening implications.

The Shake

I could be sitting in class during a lecture, walking around campus with a couple of buddies, be in the middle of a soccer game—it didn't matter. The second a negative thought about public speaking crossed my mind, I'd vibrate. Occasionally, a compassionate onlooker would turn to me and inquire, "What the hell is wrong with you?"

Even when things were going well, the trembling reminded me that I was terrified of public speaking. The depressing reality was that—as much as I wanted it to be otherwise—I was at the mercy of fear.

I was sick of experiencing the humiliating side effects, but my suffering kept my eyes on the prize. My discomfort and shame were spurring me on. I sacrificed my social life and free time to read books and watch videos on overcoming fear, but I was making a critical mistake. I believed that the books and videos would help me overcome my fears and set me on the path to a new life as a poised public speaker. Either that, or I just had to keep scouring the earth to find that magical person, book, or potion that held the key to unlocking my true potential. I was looking externally to settle my internal battles.

In that time of compulsive content consumption, I worked my butt off to make progress. I hoped and prayed that if I stayed focused and continued to gather knowledge in the months before the start of college, my college years would be party-central. I practiced public speaking constantly—I used a full-length mirror more than that guy at the gym who can't keep his eyes off his pecs.

But after reading my seventh book on public speaking in as many weeks, I realized that all my scribbles said virtually the same thing. My notes and journals, full of observations, were so repetitive, I felt I was playing that annoying "Can you find the differences between these two images?" game.

I lost hope. I'd spent so much time amassing expert knowledge—but I'd been reading the same thing repeatedly in different words. I felt like half a man. The dreams I held for my later adulthood started to appear less and less attainable. My friendly, affectionate self was **usurped** by a hangry pre-teen, pissed off at the world and at myself.

I was supposed to be having the time of my life. Instead, I became a social hermit. I redoubled my efforts and sacrificed friends and fun so I could concentrate on learning how to overcome fear. I applied many of the lessons I'd learned from the books: I practiced more, researched my audience before presentations, did breathing exercises…all to no avail. At this point, since the onset of my glossophobia, I'd had years of study and dozens of speeches under my belt, but I was still the same scared kid, petrified of standing in front of an audience.

I didn't realize it at the time, but I was doing something that many people who find themselves stuck with fear do: I was spending most of my time preparing, researching, contemplating, pondering, planning, figuring out the best way to approach this situation. I was thinking a lot, but I wasn't really doing anything.

I was down there, in that ditch, drowning.

Exercise #2: Identifying failure and fear

Every failure is a lesson—at least it should be. What lessons do you learn each time you fall short of achieving something you set your mind to? Do you apply those lessons or just try to forget the failure?

Recall your last bad presentation. What did you feel? What could you have done better to reduce the intensity of those feelings?

Exercise #3: Your Dream Speech vs. Your Average Speech

Think of your dream speech. Write your answers to the following in detail:

- How do you feel during the speech?
- How does your audience react to what you're presenting?
- What is your comfort level with the material?
- What is your level of interaction with the audience?
- Think of your average speech. Describe what you typically feel before, during, and after you conduct your presentation. Write answers to the following questions in detail:
- When do you feel the most/least stressed? What are the factors that trigger this stress?
- When are you the most confident? Why do you think this is so?
- Describe what you think you need to do, to go from your average speech to your dream speech.

PART 2

TRAINING MY MIND TO BECOME A FEAR-KILLING ASSASSIN

Note: So here we are, in Part Dos. Things are about to get wacky. In this section, we cover the most critical feature of controlling fear: the mental aspect. I'm cramming twelve years of stories and lessons into this section, all things that, had I known them early on in my struggle, would have saved me a ton of time and stress. So, buckle in, it's a wild ride....

Most chapters include a "Risk This" challenge—don't skip over these. It's also imperative that you not get impatient and skip to "The Plan." Ready? Here we go....

CHAPTER 4:

The Curse of the Over-Thinker

"You can't be that kid standing at the top of the water slide overthinking it.
You have to go down the chute."

— TINA FEY

I was wearing swimming trunks, floaties around my arms, a yellow ducky inner tube around my waist, and my 75 SPF waterproof sun screen had been applied thoroughly. Graspable ledges surrounded the pool, there was a flight of stairs just a short swim from the point of entry, two lifeguards itching to save lives were standing by, I had researched endlessly ways to avoid disaster and how to assure a successful experience in the pool, and I had Mom on speed dial just in case anything went wrong.

But instead of diving in, I stood at the edge of the pool, plotting endlessly about how I'd react to unforeseen circumstances, figuring out what I'd do every second I was in there, and concocting escape plans for when things went terribly wrong. I stood there, dumbstruck, imagining the awful things that could happen: drowning and no one noticing me; tripping and hitting my head; consuming too much chlorine and dying.

I never got those water wings wet.

Since childhood, endless plotting has been one of the main blocks in my battle against fear. Is it one of yours? Our minds tend to identify glorious opportunities, and then we crawl at precisely the moment we ought to be sprinting. We develop a plan to overcome barriers, we lay out the path, then become paralyzed when it's time to take action. This goes for everything: jumping off the high dive at the local swimming pool, acting on a great business idea, combatting fears, mastering a craft. And, when it comes to sharpening our speech-giving skills, we envision the worst possible scenarios. For example, do you worry about...

- Producing uncontrollable, nerve-induced flatulence, leaving half the room gasping for air
- Having a complete brain shutdown while you're standing on stage
- Spilling your coffee on your laptop, destroying your presentation
- Boring your listeners, causing half the room to fall asleep
- Turning so red that people mockingly suggest you are a tomato
- Misreporting information, being corrected, and looking like an idiot
- Realizing that your aunt has been obsessively trying to Skype you during your presentation—and that everyone noticed?

No wonder most of the world is terrified of public speaking! The thing is, stuff like this doesn't happen much. And if it does, it's not catastrophic. Sure, you might stumble on the way to the podium or forget what you were going to say. You might turn red, get sweaty, or mispronounce a few words. Hell, you might even shed a tear or two. But to worry that you might walk up to the stage and do something to cause irreparable damage to yourself, your ego, or your future development is a symptom of the curse of the over-thinker.

The generator of inconceivable bad thoughts that is the mind continues to formulate scenarios to keep us scared and questioning ourselves. It makes us believe that mere mortals cannot overcome the fear of public speaking. Our minds amplify all of the potential downsides until those potentialities become invincible monsters.

The pessimist side of the brain ignores the potential (and highly probable) outcomes of giving speeches. For example, speechifying can help us to:

- Gain character and emotional strength
- Take a huge step to controlling our fear
- Learn from our mistakes and grow as speakers
- Learn to inform, entertain, and enthrall a crowd
- Learn something new and have it become fully ingrained by teaching others
- Gain the ability to lead and manage
- Assist others in overcoming what's been ailing them
- Motivate, influence, and promote change
- Turn a weakness into a strength
- Impress co-workers, bosses, professors, etc.
- Create credibility
- Build a reputation
- Obtain confidence that will translate to social situations.

When we think too much, we filter out the positive and concentrate on the negative. Negativity is the byproduct of unhealthy fear—we think of and expect the worst while completely disregarding potential benefits. Like an elephant afraid of a mouse or a 6'4, 200-pound man bolting at the sight of a spider, we're all powerful creatures afraid of things we've made bigger than they really are. To protect ourselves, we keep thinking instead of taking action.

One part of the brain of this 6'4, 200-pound man with flowing bronze curls (yes, it's me) knows that in order to dispose of the spider, he has an array of options, all of which pose no physical threat to himself or his loved ones. He can grab a few tissues and flatten the arachnid, employ a fatal stomp, or toss a hard- or soft-covered book at it. He can even put on a cooking mitt and send the spider back to the deepest depths of hell with a merciless punch.

The ability to quickly analyze and take conclusive action to solve a problem that conjures fear in us is a skill that many don't ever develop. Because of this, we remain in fear. Even more problematic is that many of us (myself included, before overcoming my fear) don't recognize how simple and non-threatening some of these problems we face are to solve. From an outsider's perspective, we just look crazy. They'll offer suggestions like:

- "It's so easy!"
- "Just go for it!"
- "You're overthinking it!"
- "Why are you just standing there? You're not going to get over it unless you do it!"

- "Stop being a pansy! Get it over with!"

- "You're pathetic! You're a disgrace to humanity!" *Outsider stares at you as he insults you by doing the thing you fear over and over again with ease.*

Despite the good intentions of the speaker, this type of advice has never served as a "motivational boost." But just as an agoraphobe shouldn't sprint into a crowded shopping center, screaming "I'm free!" to defeat a fear of being trapped, and an achluophobe shouldn't descend into the Parisian catacombs to overcome a fear of the dark, it's in the glossophobe's best interest not to walk up to a podium in front of 1,000 people as the first step to overcoming fear. I've tried this "trial by fire" approach, and it set me back.

You may be wondering whether there's an antidote to this terrible curse. Well, you're in luck. The antidote is stored safely in a little crevice in your brain. To release it, there's one thing you must do: you must use hesitation as a signal to act. If you're anything like me, hesitation has always indicated that it's time to weigh the pros and cons, consider the alternatives, and finally, to make a decision. Unfortunately, by the time you make a decision, you've probably convinced yourself to take the safe route—the one with minimal risk, and minimal opportunities for growth. This, in turn, makes the antidote for the curse of the over-thinker harder to reach.

To avoid this, you need to redefine what your hesitation is trying to tell you. In other words, you need to stop assuming that hesitation means you're about to do something bad or harmful. Sure, hesitation *can* keep you from some dangerous situations, like getting into a stranger's minivan, lured with promises of unlimited lollipops; or eating a brownie that a tweaked-out teenager just handed you. But in many cases, hesitation is nothing more than a block to achieving great things. It has stopped me from doing the things I needed to do early on in my struggle to overcome my fear. It stopped me from travelling to awesome places, trying eccentric foods, and doing things that would have made me a better person, a more successful professional, and a more valiant leader.

So, take it from me: the guy who now looks back at all those times he hesitated, and only ever regrets the things he didn't do (and wishes he would have done more of the things he was scared to do). Stop pausing to consider the potential negative consequences—just act. Stop thinking, "Wait, wait, wait…I need to think this through…." No, you don't. Stop passing on opportunities just because they frighten you. DO THEM! Use your propensity to hesitate to confirm that whatever you are aiming to do is, in fact, the right thing to do. It's time to stop the never-ending formulation of the "brilliant plan" to defeat your fear. There is no plan that will work better than taking immediate action and learning from the results.

One lesson I recall every time I feel hesitant before doing something wonderful is from the movie *We're the Millers*, where Jason Sudeikis' character is inspired to share some pseudo-fatherly advice when the young man pretending to be his son fails in an attempt to kiss a girl. He recommends that when you're scared, just count to three and on three, go for it. No thinking, no second-guessing, just do it. This advice may not work for a politician, financial analyst at a Fortune 500 company, or a surgeon figuring out where to cut next. But we glossophobes need to stop pretending that every one of our decisions could have catastrophic repercussions. We just need to jump.

But sometimes, we get overwhelmed. We think, "Well, $#it. I'm really terrified. It's going to be a long, hard road to recovery...." And we start to get down on ourselves when we realize that we're here stressing out, trying to defeat a fear that most people don't even seem to suffer with. Well, there's good news for those willing to persevere: the more difficult the path, the greater the reward will be.

Risk This #1: Count to three

Next time you're about to do something that makes you nervous or uncomfortable, use the "count to three" method. Whether it's waking up early, sparking a conversation with a stranger or asking someone out on a date, just count to three and do it. Once you hit three, you better start doing it!

CHAPTER 5:

Bigger Barrier, Bigger Reward

"It is not the critic who counts; not the man who points out how the strong man stumbles, or where the doer of deeds could have done them better. The credit belongs to the man who is actually in the arena, whose face is marred by dust and sweat and blood; who strives valiantly; who errs, who comes up short again and again, because there is no effort without error and shortcoming; but who does actually strive to do the deeds; who knows great enthusiasms, the great devotions; who spends himself in a worthy cause; who at the best knows in the end the triumph of high achievement, and who at the worst, if he fails, at least fails while daring greatly, so that his place shall never be with those cold and timid souls who neither know victory nor defeat."

—THEODORE ROOSEVELT,

26th President of the U.S. (and purveyor of excellent quotes)

For most of my teenage years and into adulthood, I played in a punk rock band. I don't mean Yellowcard or Blink 182 punk rock, I mean scream-your-face-off, curse-the-government, and mosh-pit-till-you're-bleeding punk rock. I played backyard shows in East LA, South Central Los Angeles, and other dodgy locales—performing for leather-clad, spikey-haired punkers and fist-pumping gangsters, where marijuana smoke filled the air and forty-ounce bottles of Mickey's* beer and cans of Four Loko* littered the ground.

I wrote most of the music for the band—the money-bashing, cop-insulting, society-hating lyrics that often fueled the incessant pogo dancing that in turn energized our performances. I felt like a badass on the stage. The fact that at any given show, the audience might hate us and even scoff at the music we worked so hard to create bothered me, but it didn't plague my thoughts. When an audience didn't react positively to our performance, I used it as motivation to try out a few new tricks at the next gig.

It also didn't bother me that everyone in the audience was judging, watching, deciding if we were cool enough to pay attention to. On the punk rock stage, I felt comfortable. I could screw up, break a string, forget a song halfway through playing it...those mistakes only fueled me to do better next time.

Playing punk rock for a group of 300 stoners, gangsters, and teens that snuck out of their bedroom windows to come to a show in an abandoned warehouse in Boyle Heights made me feel *alive*. Having beer bottles thrown at me in the middle of a performance made me want to better my craft, or as Dad would say, "Ese ruido" (that noise). I was always nervous before performances, sometimes terrified, but it always motivated me to perform better.

But when it came to conducting a speech to a group of that same size, I'd want to crumble and die. If anyone had thrown something at me during a presentation, I would probably have broken down crying. I was nervous before presentations—often terrified. This terror hindered my performances because I couldn't stop thinking about what the audience thought of me or how nervous I looked. The idea that people were judging, watching, deciding if I was cool enough was horrifying.

Punk promoted rebelling against societal norms—like not following the predicted path of success in school and the corporate world. But I desperately wanted to succeed. I wanted to graduate with honors and give awesome presentations. I was so far away from what I wanted to become that I didn't even know where to start. But while I may have been an underachieving, confidence-torn, fear-crippled punk, I knew in my gut that if I really wanted to become a successful public speaker, I had to clear some massive hurdles.

The raucous punk rock scene gave me a certain type of courage, the screaming guitar solos made me feel gutsy, the fist-pumping, pogo-dancing audiences fed my starving self-esteem. I just needed to figure out how to transfer my raw, riotous stage presence over to the calm, collected, white-collar world of lecterns and podiums.

When we think of conducting a speech, we often become mentally incapacitated; our minds detach from logic and race to identify gigantic barriers. The means of curing terror are hidden behind seemingly insurmountable obstacles. But these obstacles may just be the keys to our success. The bigger the barrier, the bigger the reward.

In his revolutionary bestseller, *David and Goliath: Underdogs, Misfits, and the Art of Battling Giants,* Malcolm Gladwell discusses the power of obstacles in developing one's character. He describes obstacles as "desirable difficulties" and argues that the belief that a person will achieve greater things if the task is easier and the barriers are smaller is nonsense.

Gladwell reasons that there is a class of obstacles that for some people have an advantageous outcome. Also, it's not random—people who treat their obstacles as steps—not blocks—to achievement are positive people.

They know they have an extra obstacle to overcome, but they have the conviction needed to triumph.

When you listen to a successful business person or entrepreneur recount their journey to success, chances are they won't mention a rich uncle who carried them to the finish line. Instead, you'll hear how they've been beaten to a pulp, had their pride tested, and their confidence tossed in the dirt. They'll tell you how they failed continuously to overcome their massive barriers, but rose from the rubble each time they fell.

When your path to success is lined with flowers and road signs pointing you in the right direction, you don't develop the fight needed to achieve greatness. Yes, you may arrive at your destination with relative ease, but without a fight, the finish line doesn't feel all that great. When your path is riddled with ditches and barbed-wire fences, on the other hand, you're going to come out stronger, more grateful, and ready to take the world by the horns.

In any battle, a subdued effort from a self-deprecating or risk-averse rebel spells defeat. Achievers realize success because they train themselves to conquer hesitation and welcome risk. There's only so much you can achieve in your comfort zone.

Stories of Overcoming Obstacles

There are countless stories of people who have refused to allow barriers to hold them back. To inspire you, I've included a few here—dyslexics who couldn't read becoming CEOs, amputees becoming world-renowned dancers, and an impoverished single mother becoming a millionaire author—talk about empowering! Maybe these people seem hard to relate to due to their immense success, and maybe heeding lessons from the stories of now-successful individuals might not be your cup of tea. But the thing to realize is they were once in our positions, fighting to achieve a seemingly far-fetched goal, with a gargantuan barrier to overcome.

Sudha Chandran

When Sudha was seventeen years old, she was a passenger in a bus which was involved in an accident. Sudha was sitting two seats behind the driver, who was killed. With dreams of becoming a professional dancer, Sudha thought that the fracture she had suffered in her right leg would set her back a few months. Two weeks after getting her leg plastered by doctors, she went in for a scheduled check-up. As the doctors removed her cast, they quickly realized the barbaric mistake they had made: they had failed to properly clean an injury on her ankle before they put on the cast. As a result, she had to have her leg amputated to save her life.

About losing her leg, Sudha says, "I view the accident as a blessing because without it, I would be one amongst the million women who dance. But dancing with the Jaipur foot makes me one of a kind. We come to this life with a purpose. I have been a ray of inspiration to not only the disabled but also to the able. I am a real-life heroine."

Sudha suffered greatly but quickly realized that life had dealt her a blow and she must deal with it. She gave a big middle finger to lowered expectations, catapulted herself over the enormous barrier she faced, and ended up becoming a cultural icon and one of the most accomplished dancers in Indian history—as an amputee.

Marla Runyan

Runyan, as her name suggests, loves to run. She has achieved three United States 1,500 meter titles, is ranked #1 in the country in the 5K run, is a two-time Olympian and a U.S.A. Indoor 3,000-meter champion. Marla also happens to be legally blind.

At age nine, she was diagnosed with Stargardt's disease, an incurable form of macular degeneration that caused holes to develop in the membrane in the part of her eyes that are responsible for absorbing and transferring images. But Marla didn't let blindness damper her hopes of becoming a professional runner. Instead of giving up on her dream, Marla concentrated on her strengths as a runner and worked to make her weaknesses obsolete.

When walking down the street is a death-defying obstacle course, the idea of becoming a record-holding Olympian is impossible. But as Runyan has proved, it's not impossible, not by a long shot.

Christy Brown

Christy was a well-respected Irish author, poet, and painter who published many pieces, including an international best-selling novel considered to be "...the most important Irish novel since *Ulysses*" (Bernard Share, *The Irish Times*) and another that became an Academy Award-winning film called *My Left Foot*.

From the start, Christy's circumstances set him up for failure. He was one of thirteen surviving children (in his mother's twenty-two pregnancies) born into a poor, working-class family in Ireland. Shortly after his birth, it was discovered that Christy had severe cerebral palsy and complete paralysis. Consequently, doctors were forceful in their suggestions that for the sake of the family, he be committed into a convalescent hospital so he could receive adequate care. For years, he was incapable of deliberate movement and did not have the ability to speak, let alone pick up a pen to write.

When he was five, he developed the ability to move his left foot at will, and this became Christy's form of communication. The following years were spent mastering the use of his left foot and figuring out ways around his mental and physical disability to achieve everything he wanted to achieve. Christy—a man unable to move, speak, and who had an intellectual disability—managed to publish multiple, world-renowned books and become one of Ireland's most beloved authors.

Jean-Dominique Bauby

Born in 1952, Bauby was a well-known French journalist and editor of the popular French magazine, *ELLE*. At the age of forty-three, Bauby suffered a massive stroke and was thrown into a coma lasting twenty days.

Upon awakening, he realized he had lost the ability to speak. His misfortune didn't end there: Bauby's entire body was paralyzed, that is, except for his left eyelid. Instead of lying there for the remainder of his existence, Bauby remained high-spirited and, using just his left eyelid, he was able, with the help of a transcriber, to write one of the most eloquent and remarkable memoirs of our time: *The Diving Bell and the Butterfly*.

The beginning of Bauby's memoir, which he had transcribed by blinking, provides a glimpse of his amazing feat: "You survive, but you survive with what is so aptly known as 'locked-in syndrome.' Paralyzed from head to toe, the patient, his mind intact, is imprisoned inside his own body, unable to speak or move. In my case, blinking my left eyelid is my only means of communication." Damn!

J.K. Rowling

Having hit a gold mine with the *Harry Potter* series, J.K. Rowling is one of the most successful authors of all time. However, before she made it big, Rowling was impoverished and struggling to keep herself and her child alive.

After her divorce in October of 1992, Rowling fell into a deep, dark depression. She lived in a run-down, mice-infested flat in Edinburgh, Scotland, and fought to keep her daughter healthy and nourished off a $100 per week welfare check.

While struggling and fighting worsening depression, Rowling worked feverishly on the manuscript of *Harry Potter and the Philosopher's Stone*. When she finished, she sent it to publishers all over the world. One by one, publishers rejected the manuscript. However, Bloomsbury Children's Books decided to take a chance on her. When they published on June 30, 1997, the book was an instant success. J.K. Rowling became a global icon.

David Boies

David Boies is best known as the lawyer who represented Al Gore and the Democratic Party during the heated 2000 post-election battle. He has also been involved in other huge cases including representing the United States Justice Department in its lawsuit against Microsoft, New York Yankees' owner George Steinbrenner in a suit against Major League Baseball, and Napster when the RIAA sued it for copyright infringement.

Boies didn't learn how to read until the third grade and spent much of his academic career desperately straining to keep up with the written material at school. David Boies is, and always has been, severely dyslexic.

Boies' ongoing struggle with reading gave him the skills and courage to triumph over severe dyslexia—and because he shattered that barrier, the other obstacles that he had to overcome appeared to him not as giants to conquer, but instead as mere pests.

These are just six stories pulled from a library of thousands. People may argue that these are one-in-a-billion occurrences, that these journeys cannot be replicated. Others may scoff, "Roy, you're crazy. You pulled a bunch of names of celebrities with tremendous skill sets and you expect me to relate and feel motivated?" That was my reaction, too, when I first heard these stories. It didn't matter to my doubting mind at the time that there were also stories of double amputees climbing Mount Everest; people with mental disabilities accomplishing tasks that the brightest college grads consider impossible; and kids raised in impoverished circumstances developing multimillion-dollar businesses that kids with ivy league educations and CEO dads could only dream of. But I read enough of these tales to realize that there was something to all of this—and that I'd better pay attention.

I realized that these people had enormous barriers in front of them—bigger than glossophobia and bigger than social anxiety. But something happened in their lives—they all made the decision that they didn't want to be contained within those walls anymore. In order to overcome those barriers, first they needed to overcome the biggest barrier of all: their own restrictive minds. Once you realize that you have control of your mind, you gain control of your future.

Even though we glossophobes may feel hopeless, we're tremendously lucky. We're lucky because we're faced with a challenge that will test and strengthen us. Because of our fight with glossophobia—a fight we are all more than capable of winning—we will grow intellectually, mentally, and emotionally and we can build a new persona that can entertain a crowd—and at the same time, entertain us.

When I tell people who email me asking for help that there's no pill, drug, or magical potion that will do the trick, usually I don't get a response. The barrier we glossophobes face is an illusion—we are the ones that make that little spider look like a two-headed dragon and that tiny cricket look like Godzilla, we are the ones that make the public speaking obstacle into a monstrous mountain to climb. As a result, we feel that nothing we can do to overcome the obstacle will work. But—and this is critical—we can't allow ourselves to be fooled by our mind's ability to amplify these obstacles.

With a barrier in the way, achieving our goals may seem nearly impossible. But once you learn to act—instead of allowing hesitation to block your progress and caving in to your mistrust, your path will become clear. Then, nothing can stop you. In the meantime, there's one barrier that can either make you pump the brakes and reconsider your self-worth, or, it will have you sharpening the dagger that will kill your fear: *failure*.

Risk This #2: Reduce your fear with deep conversations

Go out of your way to have full-fledged conversations with three people you don't know by the end of the day tomorrow. Concentrate on keeping the conversation going and being as natural as possible. Acknowledge and aim to defeat any negative thoughts like, "What if they think I'm weird?" Secondly, concentrate on avoiding simple small talk. Instead, find and discuss matters that are of interest to the other person. If they don't want to talk to you, move on to the next person!

CHAPTER 6:

Guide to Mastering Failure

Mom: *Hijo, joo become more brave ebery time joo feel fear, and*
           act anyway. Joo must act in face of fear. Joo are stronger than joo
           think, hijo!

Me: *But Mom, how can I "act in face of fear" when I'm too scared to act?*

Dad: *I show you. Go say hi to that nena (girl).*

Me: *Heck no!*

Mom: *Por qué no?*

Me: *I'm scared! I don't know her. She'll think I'm weird. I'm not doing it.*

Mom: *No seas boludo (don't be a dummy). Close your eyes. Count to three,*
           hijo. Then go say hello. I wait here.

Me: *Omg! I feel alive!!!*

Mom: *Yes, hijo. The more you face the fear and act against its sugerencias*
           (suggestions), the more rapido (quicker) you weel realize, 'I've fought
           fear before. I can do eberything that comes my way!' Now go drink
           agua! You need eight glasses per day to estay hydrate!

Our human tendency is to avoid failure at all costs. In fact, we're so dead set on avoiding failure that we position ourselves so that we're no longer aiming for success. Sticking to the "fallible yet proud" profile of human nature, we go to excruciating lengths to avoid making mistakes, and once we do, we move mountains to erase them from our life's resume.

Question: Why are we so dead set on avoiding situations where failure is an option, when failure is such a critical piece of success? Answer: Because we're in a success-driven society that doesn't reward defeat.

We're not raised high on a platform and celebrated with confetti blasts when we get fourth place. Instead, we get insincere pats on the back and awkward "you did great, pal!" remarks. You won't find many "they failed, and that was the key to their success!" instances in the history books, because history is written by the victors. We're shown that failure is a deficiency—that failing means that somewhere along the line, we screwed up and, as a result, we are just not good enough.

But behind every success, there's a backstory of sweat, tears, and most importantly, failure. You've probably heard the story of Thomas Edison, whose prized invention, the lightbulb (arguments of whether he actually invented it aside…), took over 1,000 tries before he came through with a successful prototype: "How did it feel to fail 1,000 times?" a reporter asked. "I didn't fail 1,000 times," Edison responded. "The light bulb was an invention with 1,000 steps."

There are countless cases of entrepreneurs, athletes, and normal human beings like you and me failing to succeed. My openness to failure was a critical aspect in what ultimately led to me overcoming my fear too. The person who tries high-risk, high-reward things and experiences failures will be more creative and more willing to take the necessary steps to succeed.

I wasn't always so open to failure. Sitting at the dinner table, in my sophomore year of college, the night before a big interview for a highly-coveted internship at NBCUniversal, I spoke up to let my parents know I was thinking of bailing:

Me: Papis, I don't think I'm going to go tomorrow. I suck and I have no skills. I don't want to waste their time.

Dad: Hijo, basta (cut it out). I did not raise a cobarde (coward). Vas a ir (You will go).

Mom: No digas eso (don't say that), Roycito, joo will do fantastico, you no worry! Joo are the best!

Me: No, Mom I'm literally going to be the worst. I don't know how to do anything they're asking for on the job description. They're going to laugh at me.

Dad: Roycito, joo don't know how to do the job?

Me: Not at all.

Dad: Do joo have a brain?

Me: I guess so, yes.

Dad: Do joo have a computer joo can use?

Me: At the library, yes.

Dad: Then joo get your butt out of la cama (bed) at six a.m., joo go to la biblioteca (library), and joo use your brain to learn these things before tu entrevista (your interview). Y si la cagas (and if you screw it up), then joo will know nothing great in life comes sin sangre y sudor (without blood and tears).

Me: But Dad, I have to get plenty of rest and the computers at la biblioteca are always taken and my entrevista is at nine a.m., and...

Dad: Estop. No escusas. Figure it out. Then you go to la entrevista and do your best. If you fail, great. Then you will know you have to work twice as hard for the next one.

Me: I don't want to fail, I'm going to feel so humiliated....

Mom: Hijo, joo must learn to fail, then work harder to win the next time. Joo are a Rosell. Joo do not geev up.

Joo guessed it—I went to the biblioteca early the next morning, gathered some talking points, then somehow, someway, I rocked the entrevista and ended up getting the internship. I was pretty miserable the first week and a half on the job, though—it became clear quickly that I was in over my head. I had to conceal the fact that I wasn't quite as good at Excel, or Powerpoint as I had initially stated. But because of my oppeness to failure, I didn't give up. Instead, I studied hard, asked lots of questions, then ended up doing well.

We err when we associate failure with deficiency and being wrong with stupidity—that is simply a formula for living a highly controlled and mediocre life. Being wrong has nothing to do with intellectual inferiority or an inability to achieve. In fact, in order to continue our development, we need to recognize that the capacity to err is crucial to mental and emotional growth.

The mentality that mistakes are bad and that one must strive for perfection leads to the belief that if we just fly under the radar, avoid attention, reduce our waves to ripples, and make 'safe' decisions repeatedly, then we'll avoid getting yelled at for screwing things up. All of that probably is true—but we'll also avoid achieving anything truly remarkable.

Well, Roy, you might say, *I don't want to be the next Thomas Edison or a pioneer for global change! All I want is to overcome my fear of public speaking! All this hogwash of "make mistakes" and "failures are good" doesn't apply to me!*

You don't have to be on a mission to cure world hunger to adopt the "mistakes are positive" mindset. When the reward of success is worthwhile (in this case, learning to enjoy public speaking), accepting failure for what it is—a stepping stone—is key. It's time to start celebrating your failures. You gain confidence and become braver every time you feel fear, realize the potential for failure, and act anyways. The more you face your fear and act against its suggestions, the quicker you'll realize, "I've fought through fear before. I've failed and lifted myself up. I can do whatever comes my way."

So, the next time you forget the memory stick containing your presentation, forget what you were talking about mid-sentence, or completely butcher what was supposed to be the best part of your talk, remember that each time this happens, you take another step up the ladder to reaching your fear. The closer you get to your fear, the less power fear has over your life and your decisions. And once you meet fear face-to-face, it will finally be time for *you* to dictate the role it should have in your life.

Looking at my own list of failures so far, I realize I've messed up a whole lot but haven't always viewed failures as lessons. For example, take my life growing up as a hopeless romantic. For most of my youth and early adulthood, love evaded me. I was more of an onlooker than an active participant. I mean this literally—I would look at girls in an attempt to get their attention, and once I had obtained it, my eyes would dart downward quicker than a cricket in distress.

My mother's opinion on the matter was that there weren't any girls respectable enough for an old-fashioned gentleman like myself. She was under the impression that I was a diamond in the rough waiting to be discovered, and that I should just keep being myself and things would work themselves out. "Chicas hoy dia (girls today)," she'd say, "they are so confuse. Is a big problem. No saben lo que quieren (they don't know what they want). They look for estupid boys, sin futuro (without a future). Once they mature, las vas a volver locas (you're going to drive them crazy)." Though my father shared similar sentiments, he felt I had room to improve: "How's any chica going to be interested if your pants are tighter than hers? If joo stop wasting time making ruido (noise) with your band, you might see a chica once in a while! I have a novia (girlfriend) for you: Her name is BOOK, and joo better start spending more time with her!"

As a testosterone-fueled fifteen-year old, I didn't want to make BOOK my novia—I was more interested in warm, shapely human beings of the feminine variety. But at the time, I was too terrified of rejection to make any approaches and the ladies weren't flocking to me, so I didn't have much choice. Fortunately, Dad raised me to have the mental fortitude of a war hero. His "Oh, the shower water too cold? When I was Prisoner of War en Vietnam, I bathed with my own saliva," and his "When I left my casa in Cajamarca, Peru at thirteen years old to live on my own..." made me realize just how easy I had it. But even with a father who has experienced it all to teach me life lessons and a mother to give me the confidence I needed, I was—let's face it—a total dud.

But do you need to fail to succeed? In the pursuit of love, do you need to get rejected fifty times to figure out how to find "the one?" Concerning public speaking, must you suffer great humiliation to finally be comfortable on stage? Contrary to popular belief, no—failure is not a prerequisite for success. In fact, you don't ever need to fail to conquer your fear.

It's the same thing for those seeking love, athletic success, or a dream career—it's not about failing. You can fail 50,000 times at giving speeches and be just as likely to rock an auditorium as someone who's holding a microphone for the first time. "So," you might ask, "Why does everyone talk about failure as if it's the unavoidable stepping stone to success? Can't we just get it right the first time?"

Of course, we can! The secret isn't in failing, that is not a requirement. The key is that we must accept that our efforts could result in failure at any given moment—that with every step we take towards our goal, there exists the possibility that we will fall a few times on the way up. And we must act anyways. It's not the act of falling, it's knowing that we *might* fall, and being okay with that.

When I accepted this fact, there were situations where I fell flat on my face. I planned hilarious speeches that nobody laughed at. I tried starting conversations with people who didn't want to talk to me. I tried to look cool, but I stuttered, stumbled, and spluttered in front of audiences and made a fool out of myself more times than I can remember. But when I emerged from the emotional rubble, I came out stronger, every time. Are you aware that to achieve your goal, you have to take risks? More importantly, are you willing to take them? Say yes!

When you adopt this positive frame of mind, overcoming fear is as unavoidable as a shrieking pre-teen at an Ed Sheeran concert. You'll run into some roadblocks, sure, but you'll burst right through. On the other hand, if you want to avoid failure at all costs, maintain your dignity, and bypass any situation that will make you look bad—it's going to be a long and harrowing road.

Don't be proud that you've failed. Be proud that you considered all the pitfalls, potential negative outcomes, and anything else that could result in something undesirable, and that you were willing to do it anyways. THAT is the exact mentality you need, and it's one of the defining factors in you overcoming your fear.

So, how do you develop this mindset? One of the most critical aspects is deciphering what factors are at play in your mind with every decision you make. For me, it was Bertha and Paula—whom we'll meet in the next chapter.

Risk This #3: Go out and screw up today

Put yourself in a situation where you're bound to fail. Invite someone that looks way faster than you to a foot race, answer a question you don't have an answer to in class, ask someone way out of your league for their number...pick a situation, and go through with it.

CHAPTER 7:

Bertha and Paula

"Your faith can move mountains, and your doubt can create them."

— Anonymous

I adored them, hated them, desperately sought their attention and did everything in my power to avoid them. I even went through instances in which I wanted nothing more than to gather the courage to dump both of them from my life. I had been living every self-absorbed man's dream—as soon as I gave one of them my attention, the other did whatever was necessary to win it back.

Allow me to introduce you to Bertha and Paula.

Paula was straightforward and honest, always checking in to make sure I was taking steps to achieve my goals. Though her observations would often feel like attacks, it was only because I didn't like taking the blame for the things I was screwing up on. Paula wanted to see me grow—to get past my barriers and become the best version of myself. If I ever bailed on a presentation or skipped out on a job interview, she'd remind me that I was only hurting myself in the long run. She did everything she could to convince me to never back out of challenges.

Bertha too portrayed herself as understanding and comforting—but this only served to disguise her true intentions. Bertha was deceitful that way, and she saw my successes as threats to the health of our relationship. She strove to keep me from achieving my goals by continually looking for ways to magnify my fears and get me to accept the status quo. She pranced around gleefully when I skipped a presentation in class, and celebrated every time I convinced myself I wasn't capable of something.

You must be thinking: "Roy, I'd rather be an underpaid administrative assistant for an abusive D-list Hollywood producer than be with someone who treats me like Bertha treated you. What's wrong with you?"

Well, Bertha was the only person in my life I felt I didn't have to impress and who accepted me the way I was. She didn't make me feel bad about fabricating illnesses to skip presentations at school and she told me, "It'll all be okay," when I canceled job interviews because I was nervous. I knew she'd be happy and accept me even if ended up a loser. It was comforting.

I didn't pay much attention to Paula. She did her best to get me to spend time with her, but I couldn't. To pick Paula over Bertha in any situation caused so much backlash that most of the time, I just gave Bertha my affection to avoid the hassle. On top of that, Paula wanted to see me do well. In fact, she expected it. But to do well, I had to leave my security bubble and put myself in situations where I felt uncomfortable, suffered rejection, and experienced failure. I wasn't ready for that. So for the most part, I steered clear of Paula.

At this point, you may be thinking: "Roy, I don't understand. You seem reasonably intelligent, have a decent sense of humor and, based on your pictures on Google Images, look kind of like a young Ben Affleck. However, if you choose to continue appeasing the person that drags you to the ground instead of listening to the voice that pushes you to succeed... then I shouldn't be reading your book."

If you're thinking this, you're making a valid point. But before you leave a one-star review for my book on Amazon, let me tell you something that should make my situation more relatable. Bertha and Paula aren't real people. They exist entirely in my head. More specifically, they reside in my amygdala, the little almond-shaped part of my brain that, upon facing any challenge, dictates whether I should gather courage and fight—or flee like a petrified rat.

Bertha is the personification of Doubt, the ever-present reminder that maybe I really am not good enough to consider applying for *that* job, or that I should keep my ideas to myself because they're crappy anyways. Bertha's voice keeps my potential contained and keeps me emotionally attached to the status quo. Her way is low risk and high comfort, which is why I listened for so long.

Paula, on the other hand, is the personification of belief, the little voice in the back of my mind that constantly reminds me that I need to stop overthinking every decision, because doing so inevitably leads to procrastination and the abandoning of projects. She also wants me to not be content with being average, and to combat the fears that tightly control my potential. Her suggested way of living requires diligence and makes me vulnerable, which is why I tried to ignore her for so long.

As the years passed and my quest to overcome my fear stalled, my doubts became so dominant that any time I had a dilemma that put me outside my comfort zone, my reaction was automatic—grab Bertha by the hand and walk down Easy Street. My doubts convinced me to seek peace of mind and stay in my comfort zone, because trekking out of it for too long was too stressful.

I believed, however, that I could do better, and that I should pressure myself to start giving speeches, and doing whatever was necessary to grow. My beliefs told me I needed to get out—and stay out—of my comfort zone.

As much as I wanted to avoid these testing situations and stay in my little cave with my 'warm blankey' and a pillow fort to protect me, there was still an ember of hope burning inside me. I wanted to do the scary things that would maximize my chances of having a kick-ass future. But whenever that ember started to glow, Bertha spat on it, keeping it from igniting into a wildfire. If you have ever held back from doing something great because of fear or convinced yourself to take the easy way out, then you have felt the warm—but deceitful—touch of your own version of Bertha.

Doubt's Role in Stalling My Growth

Bertha stomped her way to center stage on that day in fifth grade when the entire classroom burst into uproarious laughter upon seeing my moobs. She introduced herself to me with a rotten smile: "Hi, I'm Bertha—I'm going to be around for a while...."

From that moment, she began to influence every decision I made. One example of her power occurred during my first internship at NBCUniversal.

NBCUniversal – Universal City, CA

Last day of internship

After nine weeks of menial grunt work, I had the opportunity to attend a "state of the company" event—all the big executives were to be present. I was elated—I arrived two hours early to prepare questions. I had a million things I wanted to ask, and made sure to research the company and the issues and opportunities it was facing.

Ten minutes before the event started, I had my list of questions ready. I was pumped. I made my way towards the conference hall. Everyone was outside socializing. I saw people I'd read about in the Business and Entertainment sections of the LA Times chatting amiably and I recalled my former self thinking, *if only I had the opportunity to be around these people, I'd be set for life.* I was about to be set for life. I smiled. But at that moment, something strange but eerily familiar happened.

It felt like a rush of frigid air blowing through my chest. Bertha had arrived. My courage froze, then shattered into a million pieces. *Now that I think of it,* I thought, *this is a REALLY big deal. I'm just a measly intern, and they'll probably get annoyed if I try talking to them. Besides, it would be rude to interrupt.*

I started to imagine all the potentially awkward situations that could occur.

Me:	"Hey, Directors of International Promotions, I'm Roy. Mind if I sit here?"
Director 1:	"Oh, I think that seat is taken."
Director 2:	"Yeah. Pretty sure it's taken."
Me:	"Okay. Thank you anyway. Have a wonderful night!" *I walk away.*
Director 3:	"That seat wasn't really taken, was it?" *Uproarious laughter.*

Producer:	*Speaking to other exec.* "My intern has been great. She's helped me so much...."
Me:	"Hey all, sorry to intrude. I'd love to know how I can improve as an intern!"
Producer:	"No, we're talking about something confidential."
Me:	"I'm sorry."
Producer:	*Turns away* "What a weirdo...."

Me:	"Hi, Ms. Marketing Director! My dream is to work in your department. Do you have any advice for me?"
Director:	"Are you asking me for a job?"
Me:	"Not at all! I was just wondering...like, what I needed to do...to be prepared for the future."
Director:	"You're asking me for a job in the future?"
Me:	"Uhhhh...."
Director:	"Goodbye."

After this whirlwind of potential outcomes had stormed through my mind, I assumed it was better to go back to my secluded spot to study my questions. *Better that than risk sounding like an idiot*, I thought.

Bertha 1, Paula 0. Round 2, START!

Following that tornado of negative thoughts, I made my way back to the conference room and picked a seat near the front. Sitting two rows behind me—alone, bored, and absentmindedly playing Tetris on her phone—was the Head of International Promotions, the exact department I dreamed of working in.

Wow, how could I get so lucky! I turned around, smiled, and opened my mouth with the intention of congratulating her on the success of one of her recent campaigns. But something all too familiar stopped me in my tracks. I immediately turned back around, and stared intently at the chair in front of me. *I can't screw this one up...this is the one person I need to impress. Yeah, I know a lot about her and the campaigns she created, but what if I sound stupid? Worst yet, what if I come across as trying to sleaze my way into her department?*

I started thinking about exactly what to say, how to phrase it, how I'd continue the conversation after her initial response, how I'd handle the potential disinterest after I revealed that I was "just an intern." After pondering the possibilities for about two minutes, the master of ceremonies came up to kick off the event—and I missed my opportunity.

Based on the amount of information I knew about the Head of International Promotions, I could have carried on a two-hour conversation.

But Bertha had stepped in and turned a completely natural situation, one that I should have been comfortable with, into a doubt-fest.

Bertha 2, Paula 0! Round 3, BEGIN!

The Q&A session was coming up. I convinced myself that the other two instances wouldn't have resulted in anything anyway and that the Q&A was my true chance to shine. I could picture it...after I asked a great question, all the executives in the room would know my name and talk to me after the event. I was relieved knowing my big moment, the one I had prepared so thoroughly for, was coming.

I looked down at my paper with scribbled notes and list of questions. The sheet was moist with palm sweat, some of the ink had begun to smear. I circled the question I had decided on—my pen stabbed through the paper, ripping the already-ravaged sheet. As the panel made their way to the stage, I held the soggy paper in my clammy hands, reading the question over and over.

"We will now begin the Q&A portion of tonight's event. If you have a question, please raise your hand and Sarah will make her way to you with a microphone."

I could feel armpit sweat trickling down my sides, resting in little puddles at my waistline. I felt my face go numb. I looked around to make sure nobody was alarmed by my sudden flush of color. My legs started to tingle, and if it weren't for the fact that I was so nervous, I'd have thought I was having a stroke. I kept asking myself: *Why the hell am I so nervous?*

The first question was asked and answered. The second question came and went. Third question. Fourth question. Each resounding "next question!" sent a jolt down my spine. *I cannot miss this opportunity...come on Roy....*

This was my final chance to make a lasting impression on the company and give myself a chance of securing a job, or at least some contacts, for when I graduated. With each passing question, I just told myself mine would be next. But when it came time to raise my hand, Bertha (Doubt) held it down. Then, I closed my eyes and took three deep breaths.

One. I began to visualize myself raising my hand, Sarah walking over with the microphone, me standing up, and proudly asking the most thought-provoking question of the night.

Two. I imagined the feelings of pride and elation that would come over me, leaving me in a state of nirvana.

Three. I imagined the mental barrier blocking my path begin to crumble.

"We have time for one more question...."

My hand shot into the air—at the same time the intern sitting two rows in front of me raised his hand.

"Yes, young man in the middle!"

Wait, me? Or him? Oh God....

The assistant commenced her trek from the back corner of the room, heading in my direction. I began to fidget. I did my best to suppress my impending panic with deep breaths and repeating, *this is NOTHING. You got this, Roy,* in my head. I vigorously wiped my hands on my pants to avoid giving her a disgustingly clammy handshake. She turned the corner and started to make her way down my aisle. I took one more deep breath.

This is it....

I felt my heart about to combust. I finally put my hand down. She was now about fifteen feet away. I half stood up, then sat back down. I got up again. We made eye contact; she smiled. I tried to smile back, but it felt as if two weights held down the corners of my mouth. I showed my teeth to signify joy, but I think I looked more like a squirrel cornered by coyotes making a last-gasp effort to scare them away.

Ten feet away, nine feet, each step felt like a kick to my stomach. Eight feet, seven. I winced as my bladder began to pulsate, sending a throbbing pain throughout my abdomen.

Six feet. Five. Suddenly, I felt a different sensation; one that I hadn't felt in a long time. I felt the fire inside of me begin to ignite. I suspect it was the sudden realization that even if I butchered my question, stuttered, or just sounded like a fool, whatever happened with that mic shoved in my face was going to be world's better than cowering. I imagined that enormous barrier again and gave it a swift kick. It fell over and shattered. I was ready.

She stopped, untangled the cord and raised the mic to my face.

"Uh, yeah, thank you for…picking mine. Hehe. This is a question, um…I have for…I mean…this question is one I have, for asking, for Mr. Bergstein." I looked up at Mr. Bergstein, expecting some sort of confirmation. He stared blankly.

I had no idea what nonsensical assortment of words and noises had just been disgorged from my mouth. I continued.

"Um, yes, okay. Bergstein. I was just wondering about, um…the company's strategy for, you know, targeting the Hispanic population…I'm Hispanic, so how will you target this growing population, like me, un hispano, haha, in the coming years…to improve ratings, do good, and grow, you know, a dedicated viewing audience?"

Wow. What a god-awful question. What a pathetic, mindless, elementary question. "Do good?" "I was just wondering ABOUT?" "UN HISPANO!?" Are you f%$^ing kidding me?!

I looked down to check if I had wet myself. I had not. I froze in place, awaiting the inevitable and humiliating, "Can you repeat that question? I didn't catch that…" or "do we have a paramedic? I think this kid is having a stroke!" *I knew I should have just kept to myself. What the hell was I thinking?*

Mr. Bergstein: "Wow, Roy…Thank you so much for that fantastic question! I know I speak for everyone up here when I say this is a critical discussion topic, and…."

I stood there, dumbfounded, a smile materializing on my face. One of the company's top executives had complimented my question and responded with enthusiasm. *Should I remain standing? Should I stop smiling?* I stared in disbelief. I felt…victorious, on top of the world. I had battled Bertha—and won.

PAULA SCORES AGAINST ALL ODDS!

I can't begin to describe the elation I'd felt at that conference Q&A. I'd risen to the occasion. I'd squandered the opportunity to speak up so many times in my life—in class, at work, in social situations—that I'd lost count. And I'd defeated Doubt. Even when I'd known answers to questions in a class, or I'd had something fantastic to contribute at a work meeting, I'd kept quiet, because of *Bertha*. And, every time I'd faced those dilemmas and elected to stay safe, I'd felt nothing but regret—until the day of the conference.

I'd tasted victory—and with that victory, I knew it was time for me to do a little more digging to figure out exactly why Bertha had so much power over me, and what I needed to do to continue lessening her power. One of those terrible habits that was empowering Bertha was a game I played that stunted my progress. It's called "the blame game" and in the next chapter, I'll explain the rules—I'm sure you've played it too!

Risk This #4: Reliving regretful decisions

Think of three situations where you held back from doing something you now regret not doing. What happened in your mind as you were deciding whether to act on those things? Now, reimagine those situations as if you had done the opposite. What is the result?

Next time you are in a similar situation, keep in mind that fear is a signal for action, NOT withdrawal, and remember your regrets from past situations.

Risk This #5: Meet an Idol

Whether it's at your school or at the company you work for, find one person you've always wanted to meet but never conjured the courage to approach. This could be a top-level executive, the President of a university, or just a colleague/peer you've always wanted to talk to. Once you decide who that person is, approach them and start a conversation.

CHAPTER 8:

The Blame Game, and Weakening Bertha

"I've got 99 problems and 94 of them are completely made-up scenarios in my head that I'm stressing out about for absolutely no logical reason."

— ANONYMOUS

When we were little kids, my brother and I often played a game. It would start with us kicking a soccer ball around the living room, passing it around until we got dizzy. Eventually, one of us would slam the ball into Mom's favorite lamp, or it would ricochet off the awkward family photo hanging on the wall, or something else would get broken. We'd cringe and cover our ears as the sound of shattering glass resonated throughout the house and the approaching screams of "Que paso? Que rompiedon (What did you break)!?" made our little hearts nearly burst out of our chests. Then, the game would begin.

Me: "It was Pablo's fault! He can't aim for beans!"

Pablo: "Nuh uh, it was stupid Roy! His boney leg made the ball hit the lamp!"

After hearing our desperate cries of innocence, Dad would interject:

Dad: "Ah, okay Roycito. Es culpa de Pablito, no (it's his fault)?"

Me: "Si! Si! Papa he sucks at aiming! Es su culpa!"

Dad: "Okay, Pablito. Answer my question, por favor. Es culpa de Roycito, no?"

Pablo: "Yes! Yes! Papa his stupid boney leg made the ball hit the picture, I swear!"

Dad: "Okay, perfecto! Both of joo are to blame! Now clean this up ahora, carajo (now, damn it)!"

This early habit of blaming others for things I was fully responsible for evolved into a whole array of finger pointing, which lasted into my third year of college. I blamed:

- A professor's accent for a D in Statistics
- A D in Statistics for a C in Business Calculus
- Inconsiderate teachers for my bad GPA in high school
- Genetics for my inability to get in shape
- A failing economy for my inability to find internships
- Living in the wrong era for my difficulty in making new friends
- Luck not being on my side for my misfortunes
- Luck being on everyone else's side for their successes
- Genetics, inconsiderate teachers, acne, a subpar self-esteem, and living in the wrong era for my inability to overcome the fear of public speaking.

The blame game was just one of many activities the negative forces in my mind played to keep me unmotivated. I'd blame everything that went wrong for me on something outside of my control. However, I discovered later on in life that if I ever wanted to overcome my apparent aversion to success, I had to stop playing the blame game.

It took some time for me to realize this, but it finally hit me at the end of my second year of college. It came after overhearing a conversation between two of my peers after we all received our final exam scores:

Mark: "Oh, my God…I got a D. That final was so pathetic. That professor is so stupid and can't teach for s^%t."

Peter: "I got a D too. This is her fault, she didn't even teach these concepts properly!"

Mark: "She's the worst! I can't believe we're failing this class because of her."

Peter: "Yeah. Plus, why would she schedule this class at 8:00 a.m.? We can't think straight this early!"

As I listened to this conversation, I started to feel disgusted. They were blaming their terrible grades on everything except the fact that they hadn't studied, or that they didn't seek help on concepts they didn't comprehend, or that maybe, they just didn't try hard enough.

Then, I realized that I had been doing the exact same thing. I was blaming everything and everyone but myself for many of the things that weren't going my way—particularly my fear of public speaking.

After realizing this, I became more selective with my blaming. Instead of pointing a finger at a bad professor for a crappy grade on a French

Grammar midterm, I blamed myself for not putting in the effort to speak French every day. Instead of blaming incompetent bosses for my inability to progress quickly in my career, I blamed the fact that I didn't work hard enough to sharpen my leadership qualities and my knowledge of the industry. I shifted my focus from external blaming to internal blaming.

And with that, I finally began to taste progress.

By shifting my blame, I saved all the time and effort I'd usually spend on seeking a scapegoat. Instead of explaining, reasoning, and digging for things to cling to to explain my gross inability to move forward, I took responsibility and sought solutions that I could actually act on (not excuses I had no control over).

So, if I screwed up on a midterm, regardless of how intelligible the professor's accent was or how terrible their teaching style, I knew I had to study harder next time. If I played a bad soccer game, I knew I had to train harder for the next one, not complain about how muddy the field was or how poorly my teammates played. I started to make big changes in the way I justified my screw-ups. As a result, I felt much more in control.

Bertha became desperate. She tried to be so sweet in convincing me things weren't my fault. "Wait, Roy, no! It's not your fault you failed that test! You don't need to do anything different, that professor didn't know what they were doing!" ... "Roy, don't stress. That terrible performance review has nothing to do with you. Your boss is just an a-hole who has it out for you!" ... "Roycitoooo, it's okay that you didn't do well in the speech. Maybe you should take a break from public speaking. Stop trying so hard!"

So, here's the good news: You don't need to play the blame game anymore. You are solely responsible for your luck, self-esteem, GPA, professional future, and your phobias. The outcome of the mental battles you face, the fears you're trying to overcome, and the mountain you're itching to climb—it's entirely on YOU.

People resort to blaming when overcoming an obstacle gets too difficult. It's a defense mechanism—I mean; why wouldn't you want to take the heat off yourself? Nobody likes being seen as weak—or worse yet, a failure. But blame is a knee-jerk defense mechanism that kicks us completely off track. Taking responsibility for your disappointments and finding a way to traverse that mountain takes guts, and more importantly, it takes trust. Trust that this pain will lead to victory. Trust in the process. Trust that, even though there is nothing signaling that you will succeed, no easy path leading you to the summit, you should keep on fighting, knowing that these failures will eventually lead to victories.

So, how do you get rid of the blame game mentality? First off, you need to know that what fuels the blame machine is Doubt (Bertha), and hesitation, so learning how to recognize and reconcile Doubt, and to quickly redefine hesitation is critical. Even though most people don't give names and detailed physical characteristics to the voices in their heads, everyone has their version of a *Bertha*—the voice that blames shortcomings on external factors, deflects responsibility, and makes you complacent. Your Bertha is the voice that pushes you to deflect responsibility.

Likewise, everyone has their version of a *Paula*—that inner voice that drives you towards achievement, reminds you that you're capable and keeps your head up when the going gets tough. This voice makes you responsible for your own destiny.

Both voices are a part of you—you create them, you decide how much power to give them, and you choose which of them to listen to in any given situation.

We all need to realize that we'll never avoid internal decision-making battles. Everyone must go through them. As I noted earlier, during my own twelve-year battle, Bertha had controlled my thoughts and actions, and was always standing at the ready with great excuses. After years of letting her have the upper hand, I found the key to ending that destructive relationship, and it all started with that defiant act against her at the "state of the company" conference at my internship with NBCUniversal. Bertha had done everything in her power to stop me from asking a question, but I did it anyway. And even though everything in me was telling me it was going to go terribly wrong I took a risk—and I emerged victorious.

I weakened Bertha—and with that, she lost her role as the primary decision maker in my life.

Once she'd lost her front and center status, Bertha was like a violent, possessive ex. (Today, she has accepted that she's no longer deciding for me what I can and can't do, so she sits in a dusty corner of my mind, mumbling unhelpful and discouraging phrases, hoping that I'll heed her directives and revert back to my old, fearful self.) Finally, I was becoming the Roy I'd always dreamed of being—and I was on my way to leaving the anxious, sweaty, terrified Roy behind.

Once I'd limited Bertha's power, the peak became visible through the clouds and the treacherous cliff side that had once seemed impossible to scale felt like a simple uphill walk. I knew what I had to do and, for the first time in my life, I knew I was capable of doing it. But I had to be careful of giving Bertha the space to jump back in.

The battle with Bertha is never over. Even after consecutive victories over her, she can still sneak back in to your decision-making process to confuse and scare you. Three months before my commencement speech at Cal Poly Pomona, she nearly convinced me to do something that could have ruined me. I'll tell you about that little Bertha maneuver in the next chapter.

Risk This #6: Kill Your Excuses

List three situations where you failed to go through with something because of your fear. List the justifications you used to convince yourself that backing out was okay. Now, pick one of those situations and set a deadline of the end of the week to achieve it. Remember your justifications and use them as a reminder to achieve that goal this time.

CHAPTER 9:

The Decision That Changed My Life

"Hope is the only bee that makes honey without flowers."

— ROBERT GREEN INGERSOLI

Recall that before I learned to control my fear, I blamed my inability to defeat glossophobia on a genetic disposition—taking the responsibility off my shoulders and placing it squarely on factors outside of my control. I was like the terrified teenager in horror films who hides under the bed, hoping the machete-wielding murderer gets bored, goes home, and starts a new life as a cotton candy salesman. My father didn't take too kindly to being blamed for my limitations.

Dad: "Roy, estop it. When I was a prisoner of war in Vietnam...."

Me: "I can't, Dad. I've already tried everything. It's genetics. Not my fault."

Dad: "Oh! Genetics! So, mi culpa, eh? Escuses, escuses...I have given over 100 speeches y tu mama speaks to classrooms every week, y tu abuelo, he was a great...."

Me: "Dad, stop! It's not my fault! I'm serious, it's not my...."

Dad: *Storms to my room to confiscate my Game Boy.*

As much as I wanted to be a great speaker like my outspoken abuelo and decorated Vietnam war veteran father, I just couldn't get myself to estop making escuses. I had taken several steps to overcome my fear, but they weren't all steps forward. I'd given solid presentations, but almost always followed them up with a several-month hiatus from public speaking. I'd crushed Bertha, only to invite her back in to heal her wounds later.

Without realizing it at the time, I had adopted a dangerous "victim" mentality. I fought my fear, I sought change, but conveniently, I always took the path with the least trials and tribulations. That path twisted, turned, and led me right back to where I'd started—every time.

I didn't realize I had adopted this victim mentality, and that I wasn't paying attention to the glaring signs. I was:

Placing blame. I blamed anything and anyone but myself. It wasn't my fault I had this fear. It was the circumstances I found myself in. Or the people around me that didn't offer their support. Or a lack of money to pay for classes to cure me. Or....

Being passive. When I faced a challenge, I didn't rise to the occasion to face it or start to brainstorm ideas to conquer it. Instead, I took a nonchalant, "whatever happens, happens" approach.

Deflecting power. I undermined my own ability to make the necessary changes to my current attitude, so I wasn't actively looking for solutions to implement. Instead, I gave that power to factors I couldn't control.

The victim mentality blocked my progress. When I read books or watched videos on the subject, I came away with little more than a bunch of notebooks filled with scribbles. Sure, the books helped me give better speeches—I upgraded from reading my speeches word for word, to ad-libbing to fill in the gaps. I learned how to make a good PowerPoint deck, how to use hand gestures in a concise manner (no longer did I look like the wacky, Inflatable-Arm-Flailing-Tube-Man at car dealerships), and I learned techniques to keep an audience intrigued. But my victim mentality didn't allow me to absorb and take action on the lessons I'd learned. When content absorption didn't cure me, I didn't take action to figure out how I could implement everything I'd learned. My reaction was: *These authors don't know what the hell they're talking about! These books are garbage!*

The Decision That Changed My Life

Three months before the big speech

I was twenty-three years old, with the emotional fortitude (and the hair) of a lamb before shearing season. At the time, the idea of jumping into a vat of poisonous water spiders sounded less terrifying than giving a ten-minute presentation to my peers. On nights before speeches, I pictured sheep jumping fences to lull me to sleep, but every time, an army of poisonous spiders would launch a savage attack, killing the sheep, and any chance of a good night's sleep for me. Over eleven years of suffering, I still hadn't managed to control my fear of public speaking. Or spiders.

So, I did what most people who continuously fall short of achieving their goal do…I gave up. I deemed myself a lost cause, doomed to roam the earth unfulfilled. I wasn't a complete failure, though. On the bright side, I had made progress, even though I was a long way from the goal I had set of loving public speaking by the time I graduated college. In fact, I hated public speaking. Then, three months before grad—and in the midst of my public speaking terror, I received a call.

"Hello, may I speak to Roy?"

Yes, Roy here!

It was the office of the Dean of the College of Business at Cal Poly Pomona. Dread seeped in, a malevolent fog. I'd spent five years at Cal Poly fabricating medical emergencies on speech days and crafting convincing arguments to convince professors to boost my grades—so I braced for the worst.

"Is this a good time?"

A lifetime of facing disappointment has taught me that when someone asks if it's a good time, it's usually another way of saying, "I'm about to give you some soul-crushing news, prepare yourself." My anxiety rose to a whole 'nother level. I trembled violently, panic hit me like a soccer ball to the nuts.

I lied. *Sure it is!* I coughed, nearly choking on the thick saliva clogging my throat. *Just say it!* I thought. *Just put me out of my damn misery!* I started to predict all the possibilities: *They have video footage of me stealing chicken nuggets from the commissary? One of the equestrian team's horses was stolen and I was the prime suspect? They realized I wasn't, as I claimed, really recovering from pneumonia, chickenpox, mononucleosis, rabies, or gastroenteritis all those times I skipped classes on presentation days early in college?*

"The College of Business and the President of Cal Poly Pomona has voted you as the President's Scholar for the 2013 graduating class for your outstanding academic achievement, exemplary leadership, and community involvement. You will be recognized along with the Valedictorian at commencement. On behalf of Cal Poly Pomona, congratulations!"

Denial. Confusion. Elation. Holding back tears. *My parents are going to be so proud.* I was on Cloud Nine and nothing could get me off. The worries about my future and the overwhelming disappointment about not being able overcome my fear dissipated.

"Oh! There's one more thing...we need you to give the presentation. Just seven minutes or so. You'd be the only student speaking, so this is your chance to fully embody the student experience for everyone."

Click!

I flung my phone across my room. From Cloud Nine to the depths of hell in a sentence. I was in agony. I came up with four different excuses to bail from that speech. I settled on blaming faulty reception for the dropped call, asking when graduation was, then informing the Dean that I'd be in Argentina visiting family during that time. Moments later, the phone rang.

"Roy?" said the voice on the other line, with an air of concern.

Before I could explain the dropped call and begin my desperate reasoning, I muttered two words that would change my life forever: *I'm in.*

The rest is an indistinguishable blur. A million thoughts ran through my head, none of which resembled the elation I had experienced when I was first notified of the award. I had just received the most incredible news, the opportunity of a lifetime—but it came with my worst nightmare attached. I couldn't even begin to fathom the agony, sitting up there on the stage with all the dignitaries, the minutes before presenting ticking past, the tortuous seven minutes during which I would crash and burn.

Bring on the army of spiders.

I wasn't entirely sure where that voice that said *I'm in* came from, but I had a sneaking suspicion that it was Paula, that part of me that knew I was capable of anything I set my mind to. And that kneejerk reaction that caused me to chuck my phone across the room and contemplate excuses to not attend graduation? Bertha, of course, the generator of doubt and promoter of risk-avoidance.

I wanted to find that voice of belief and make it my own. I recognized it from other times in my life when incredible opportunities arose, but I didn't always listen to it. I knew that finding that voice would be critical to my success.

At that precise moment, I made myself two promises: I would spend the next three months doing everything in my power to get comfortable with public speaking, and I would give the best graduation speech that Cal Poly Pomona had ever heard. The decision to act in the face of fear—to accept the challenge even though everything in my being was telling me I was inept—was my catalyst. I'd suffered for eleven years and had nothing to show for it. Three months of persistence later, I was free of fear's grasp.

There were a lot of things I had to do in those three months to succeed, especially mentally. One of those things was redefining fear.

Risk This #7: The Victim Mentality

Think about a recent failure you've experienced (for instance, not getting that work promotion you deserved or not passing an exam at school). List things you could have done better to increase your chances of succeeding at that task or challenge. Be as detailed as you can.

Consider that recent failure—what were your expectations before you actually failed? Were you positive, negative, neutral? Cautiously optimistic? Describe your thoughts and emotions prior to the outcome.

CHAPTER 10:

Redefining My Fear

"I realized fear is nothing more than a glass barrier waiting to be shattered because it's fear that sets limitations, that makes us complacent, that justifies excuses, that does not allow us to be extraordinary."

—ROY ROSELL (yup, I'm quoting my commencement speech)

When people describe their deepest fear, they'll often say, "I was scared to death." Death and public speaking often come up in the same conversation. If you asked me what it is about death that makes me uncomfortable, I'd tell you about my mother's broken heart, my father's despair, and my brother picking up the slack for all the unrealized potential left in the family. I'd tell you about the empty desk at the front of the classroom where I once sat, with a flower on its chair, and people I'd never had a conversation with, tears streaming down their faces falsely proclaiming, "I lost a great friend today"—as I stare down (or up) in disbelief. I'd talk about the undeserving dimwit who would take the job I've been working my whole life to obtain. I'd go on to talk about opportunities lost, potential unmet, and my overwhelming feeling of disappointment.

If you asked me what it is about public speaking that makes me uncomfortable, I'd tell you about my mother's broken heart, my father's despair, and my brother picking up the slack for all the unrealized potential left in the family. I'd tell you about my empty desk at the front of the classroom on the day of a presentation, where I should be awaiting my chance to present. Instead, my friends and classmates will falsely proclaim, "Roy is sick today," as I sit at home, playing FIFA on my Xbox, feeling like a total screw-up. I'd tell you about the undeserving dimwit who would take the job I've been working my whole life to obtain because I couldn't handle the presentation requirement. And I'd go on to talk about opportunities lost, potential unmet, and my overwhelming feeling of disappointment.

As farfetched as it seems now, there were times in my past where I looked down at my weekly schedule, saw it riddled with required speeches, and thought:

"I have a speech in a week? Just kill me now…."

"I'd rather drown in a vat of spider blood than conduct another speech…."

"I have a presentation tomorrow? Ending my life immediately."

People will declare to the four winds that they'd rather jump off a cliff, swallow a live crab, or consume a bottle of laxatives than give a short presentation to their classmates. There is even a 1973 R.H. Bruskin Associates' survey published in David Wallechinsky, Irving Wallace, and Amy Wallace's book, *The Book of Lists* that concluded that the fear of public speaking is the greatest fear for forty-one percent of people—more than death and sickness combined. More than escalators, elevators, darkness, ghosts, and the apocalypse combined. More than being tossed in a cave filled with human-eating vampire bats and acid-spraying spiders. More than—you get the point.

Whether you see death, self-mutilation, or the consumption of live insects as a viable alternative to the podium, we can mostly agree about one thing—public speaking is harder than it should be. So why in the world would something so simple be a joy for one person, but the fear equivalent of being thrown into a poisonous insect's nest for another?

My fear made me miserable, but for a long time I couldn't put my finger on what I was so scared of. I knew how it made me feel: an agonizing emptiness in my stomach, an unleashing of sweat, an urge to urinate—sometimes nausea. I could easily define that. I was willing to do whatever was necessary so people wouldn't suspect I was terrified: I'd soothe my trembling voice, stand behind an object to conceal my shaking legs, and fiddle with something to ease the tension. And what would I do when I felt the fear rising in me? Freak out. When on stage, my mind would run wild with prognostications of all the horrific things that could happen. My skin would go even paler, my stomach would tighten, and my mind would wander to the deepest depths of Hades. *What the hell was I so afraid of?*

For most of my life, I also had a fear of death. I knew that on the day of my birth, death had begun its long trek towards me, certain to one day reach its destination. I feared loss: I knew that once the light went out, it would be darker than if it had never shone. I feared heartbreak: the idea of giving someone my heart, only to have it returned to me in a thousand pieces. Moreover, I feared spiders: they are earth-bound demons that must be banished to the underworld.

With public speaking, I feared something that wasn't real, or that even made any sense. I feared that my reputation would be destroyed if I stuttered, that my self-worth was at risk every time I stood in front of an audience. I feared that I'd be judged, categorized, ridiculed for something I'd do on that stage. I had a haunting suspicion that whenever I had a presentation, there was a high probability that something catastrophic would happen.

Before learning to control my fear, I didn't know that even if I stuttered, trembled, forgot my speech in its entirety or stood on stage like a fool for ten minutes without muttering a syllable, I'd be just fine. I didn't know this because, as humans, our brains can't tell the difference between a real threat (a clutter of spiders about to attack) and an imagined threat (peers watching us). Our inability to distinguish between the two causes us to treat fear as a signal to protect ourselves from harm. I fought so hard to conceal my true sentiments from other people, but my fear level would skyrocket when I did. I'd still be self-conscious and my presentation quality took a hit. Instead of fighting, I'd throw up the white flag and plead for mercy, allowing fear to get a tighter grip.

To overcome my fear sooner, I needed to reverse this way of thinking. I had to stop believing that feeling fearful always meant there was an impending threat, and I had to stop wasting energy trying to conceal it from others—and from myself. More importantly, I had to *redefine* the emotion that consumed me every time public speaking was introduced into a conversation.

So, what do you do before a speech when your palms get sweaty, your heart starts to race, and the pressure in your stomach intensifies? You must recognize and manipulate that emotion to propel you forward. Instead of escaping it, empowering it, or pretending it doesn't exist, you must look it in the eye, grab it by the hand and say, "I'm not in danger. We're going to do this my way." When you master this ability, your fear loses its control over you.

The first step to doing this is to understand that when it comes to public speaking, fear is just trying to trick us in to believing we're about to do something dangerous.

Reality	Fear Goggles
Ask someone out on a date.	Risk being single for rest of life, own twenty-seven cats.
Quit job you despise for a new venture.	Secure future of homelessness/rotten teeth.
Give a speech to group of twenty colleagues.	Wrap body in bacon, walk into lion's den.

Whenever we're about to do something that will help us grow, our fear kicks in and tries to convince us not to do it. The reality is, when it comes to public speaking, every opportunity is a chance to do something extraordinary. Fear should serve as a signal that *excites* you, not *paralyzes* you.

You may be thinking: "Okay Roy. I've read hundreds of these motivational catchphrases that are supposed to inspire me, but they're just words...I need proof that 'redefining my fear' is something I can actually do."

Before learning to control my fear, I was in the same boat. I hated being told by my parents, "Believe and joo can achieve, hijo!" or "Reach for the estars and you weel land en de cloud!" These corny, cure-all phrases that were supposed to help just made me sneer. How was I supposed to apply these big ideas? It's true that many such sentiments are vague and don't come with an instruction manual, so they aren't exactly actionable. Unless we figure out how to act on them, they're just words.

But when it comes to redefining fear as motivation, these fluffy, insanely corny, inspirational phrases that make you roll your eyes, must become your state of mind. Everything from "use fear to propel you" and Mom's "joo must believe," are a requirement for progress in redefining your fear. The end goal is to use those pesky nerves we feel before and during our presentations to benefit us.

Research conducted by Dr. Jeremy P. Jamieson at the University of Rochester, Dr. Wendy Berry Mendes at UCSF, and Dr. Matthew Nock at Harvard University sought to answer the question, "Can we actually use nervousness to our advantage?" To figure this out, the research team invited two groups of participants to take part in their study.

After arriving at the lab, the first thing participants did was rest quietly for five minutes so an accurate baseline recording of their biological signals could be measured. After getting the baseline measurement, the speakers were asked to conduct a taped, five-minute speech about their strengths and weaknesses to two evaluators. As part of the experiment, the evaluators were instructed to display negative, non-verbal feedback (like frowning, brow furrowing) throughout the speech.

Before presenting, the participants split into one of two groups. Both groups were a mix of individuals with social anxiety disorder (SAD) and those without it.

The experimental group: These people were educated on the functionality of stress, the sympathetic nervous system, and how acute stress responses aids performance. The goal of this was to encourage participants to reinterpret stress as excitement. By highlighting all of the good things that stress can do, the doctors hoped that signs of stress arousal, like sweaty palms, racing heart, the need to pee, etc., would trigger a more positive emotion during their five-minute speech.

The control group: No instructions were given prior to presenting.

Confronted with the extremely stressful public speaking situation, both SAD and less anxious participants from the experimental group unanimously had better outcomes compared to subjects in the control group. They felt better prior to presenting, had less or no negative thoughts during their presentations, were satisfied afterwards, and their cardiovascular systems pumped more blood to their brains, allowing them to give better speeches than participants in the control group. Surprisingly, there was no difference in cardiovascular functioning between the SAD participants and the less anxious individuals.

We all can reinterpret stress or fear as excitement, but we have become so accustomed to reacting negatively to any indicator of stress that the go-to emotion is *negative*. For me, stress always signaled an impending panic attack—and the moment I felt nervousness, I would:

- Contemplate different strategies to reduce my nervousness as much as possible.

- Think of every way to conceal my nervousness so no one would notice.

- Think of ways to avoid whatever I feared.

Then, in "those three months," I switched it up. I stopped scrambling for ways to reduce my nervousness. I stopped trying to hide that I felt nervous. Instead, I decided to embrace it. No more repeating, "I am calm, this will all be over soon" to myself. From that moment on, I started saying, "I am excited, and this is going to be awesome." The feeling of "Uh-oh..." became "Oh yeah!"

This tiny change made a world of difference. Halfway through those three months, I hit an emotional gold mine. My fear became a superpower—whereas before it hindered me, now it drove me to excel. The nervousness before presentations was still there, but the negativity I typically felt was not. Excitement and eagerness replaced dread and avoidance. I realized that as soon as I felt my heart racing and negative thoughts started to seep into my mind, I could interrupt the fear response with a quick, deep breath and a rational thought, "This isn't dangerous. This is awesome!" The fear of public speaking is simply a misfiring of the "fight or flight" fear response—we just have to practice our aim.

But redefining my fear wasn't the only thing I had to do...Oh no.

Another critical aspect to learning to control my fear had to do with managing those sneaky, negative thoughts that always seemed to squeeze themselves into my mind whenever things weren't going so well (and even when they were). I had to work on eliminating those thoughts that brought me down.

Risk This #8: No bad feelings

Whether it be a speech, a job interview, or a date, think of a time that you had the opportunity to do something that made you feel fear, but you elected not to do it. Then, respond to the following:

Write down a description of all the bad things you were imagining that could happen. Separate each potential outcome with bullet points.

Look at everything you listed for number 1 and ask yourself: are these valid concerns, or fabrications of your fear to keep you from doing something awesome?

Now, write down all the positive things that could have happened had you taken action.

Risk This #9: Defeating excuses

Think of the last time you were nervous before a speech and write down five reasons why you think you were nervous. Now, write down a "defeating excuse" next to each reason you listed. Realize that every "reason" you come up with for not being able to give a speech is nothing more than a self-defeating excuse. Next time you go up to speak, remember your list of five excuses and don't allow yourself to use them.

CHAPTER 11:

Defeating Self-Defeating Thoughts

"When something goes wrong in your life just yell 'PLOT TWIST',
and move on."

— MOLLY WEIS

s glossophobes, we tend to scoff at the idea that our minds have
the power to "redefine" emotions or "conquer" fears. Many of us
will argue that we have tried to be positive and we're convinced
that there's no way we'll learn to redefine our fear without some kind of
magic pill or brain-altering procedure.

Before writing this chapter, I wanted to speak to people who share this
fear and ask them why they haven't been able to reduce their anxiety to a
manageable level. You can learn a lot about your struggle by just asking
yourself, "Why can't I get over my fear?" I wanted to confirm my theory
that glossophobes share a pessimistic view of their struggle, which deters
their ability to take the necessary steps to overcome it.

I spoke to 130 people—ninety college students and forty early to
mid-career professionals. This may not sound like a huge group, but I
didn't have an agency or team to conduct this research—I was a one-man

data-gathering machine, relentlessly pestering young adults to provide me with information they weren't comfortable sharing. At first, I started gathering my data online, through emails and hopefully not-too-creepy Instagram and Facebook messages.

After getting a few results, I wasn't satisfied. I wanted to get a sense of each person's reactions to the questions, not just their words. I scrapped that method of data-gathering and elected instead to make it more personal by approaching people at school, at work, and in public places.

Once I'd exhausted my list of friends and colleagues, I started asking strangers. I felt like those people you see on the streets with little informational pamphlets and credit card swiping devices, inquiring, "Do you have a minute to save the pandas from going extinct?" or, "If ten dollars could save this child from starvation, would you pitch in?" Aside from the guilt and moments of self-reflection that come with saying "No" to these questions, it's not hard to ignore these guys. When you're on the receiving end of those dismissive nods and irritated side glances, you gain a whole new appreciation for these street warriors.

After a brief intro, I kicked off my research with a question to help me filter the responses: "Do you have a fear of public speaking?" Only two people (both from the working professional's category) gave me a definitive "No" answer, and twelve gave me a "kind of, but not too bad" type of response (six students, three working professionals). For these two groups of responders, that was the extent of my questioning. For the 116 individuals that expressed having a fear of public speaking, I had the chance to figure out why they still hadn't overcome their crippling fear.

I asked the 116 individuals a second question: "Why haven't you been able to overcome your fear yet?" I got three types of responses.

Don't know how (57 people). The responses in this category ranged from "I don't know where to start..." to "I've tried everything others suggest but nothing works!"

Don't have time (35 people): These respondents admitted to having a fear of public speaking, but assumed that the process required to get over it wouldn't fit into their busy schedules.

Don't have the courage (24 people). Responses like, "Well, I know that to get over my fear I just have to do the thing I fear, but I just can't bring myself to do it" were most common in this category.

Whether it's due to a lack of time, a lack of knowledge, or a lack of courage—there is a unifying theme to all of these excuses. No matter how hard they try, people don't trust that they can control their fear. That was certainly true for me. Over twelve years, I attempted many strategies to help ease my anxiety—but none of them were the 'magic pill' I was looking for. I tried:

Yoga	Breathing exercises
Practicing more	Obsessing less
Therapy	Meditation
Visualizing "I'll give a great speech!"	Using notecards
Not using notecards	Imagining that the audience is naked
Imagining that the audience is non-existent	Focusing on one person in the audience
Imagining I'm a model	Imagining I'm the President

Taking a shot of liquor	Taking six shots of liquor
Including the audience	Being open about my nervousness
Trying to disguise my nervousness	Exercising brevity
Winging it	Convincing myself that failure is okay.

Yep, I tried it all. But after years of trying the same things, I started to notice that it didn't really matter how hard I practiced, how great my PowerPoint slides were, what I pretended my audience consisted of, or how plastered I got prior to presentations. I only started to see a big difference when I concentrated my efforts on:

- Visualizing, "I'll give a great speech!"
- Convincing myself that failure is okay
- Practicing more
- Including the audience.

The power of visualizing success was popularized for the twenty-first century by Rhonda Byrne's bestseller *The Secret* and enforced by Norman Vincent Peale's *The Power of Positive Thinking*, Pam Grout's *E-Squared*, and countless other books on the subject. People credit positive thought for getting them promotions at work, curing life-threatening diseases, and an endless list of seemingly miraculous achievements. I'm not one to tell you that you'll be able to use your mind to get an Aston Martin in your driveway, though many will say this is possible too.

What I will tell you is this: An unwavering belief in yourself and your ability to control your fear and give great speeches is a powerful weapon. This way of thinking discards excuses, and puts you in a mental state primed for achievement.

For a majority of the twelve years I struggled with glossophobia, I also struggled with self-doubt. But towards the end of my battle, when I started to chip away at my self-doubt, the other strategies finally started to work for me. With the knowledge that I had the tools to overcome my fear, practicing became the fuel to reach the heights I now trusted were attainable. I just had to have that base of unbreakable confidence that "I will succeed" for all these strategies to have their desired effects.

But as I inched closer to achieving my goal, there were instances that would have had me sprinting off the stage bursting into tears had I not nailed down a belief in myself. The most notable of the bunch was a speech I gave early in my fourth year of college, where I decided to try to be conversational onstage.

Conversational Catastrophe

Senior year at Cal Poly Pomona – upper division marketing class

I walked up to the podium. A thick bead of sweat trickled down my spine. I'd had intense pressure in my stomach for an hour—it became unbearable. I was insanely, inexplicably nervous, and no matter how deeply I breathed or how many times I whispered, "It's going to be okay, buddy," I couldn't calm myself. I could feel my heart struggling to pump the blood necessary to sustain me, and it seemed like I would soon collapse.

It was getting impossible to conceal my level of panic, but I managed to stand up and scan the room for five seconds. I planted a stupid smirk on my face—a desperate attempt to convince the audience that I was feeling confident.

I dove in.

"Hello class, have you ever heard about what is the 4 P's of marketing is?" Yes, you read that correctly—I'd said, "...heard about what is the 4 P's of marketing is" in front of a packed classroom. In fact, I'd yelled it because I'd just read an article that having a strong, clear, and distinguished vocal tone was an attractive trait. For some reason, my "strong, clear, and distinguished" voice came out sounding like I was hosting bingo night for half-deaf senior citizens...slow and obnoxiously loud.

I stopped. *Seriously? Did I really just say that?* Not a single person answered my question, so after an excruciatingly awkward pause, I was forced to respond to my own question with my scripted, "Well, that's fantastic! But did you ever know about there is a five P?"

F%#k. My. Life.

I decided it was time I looked up at the audience to satisfy the "make eye contact with your audience often" requirement for a good speech. Before me sat a sea of confused, concerned, and—I admit—disgusted faces. Confused because they didn't know what the hell I was asking; concerned because some of them thought I might be having a stroke; disgusted because they were attending the same educational institution as someone who apparently had the intellectual capacity of a lake trout.

If this had happened at a time in my life when I didn't accept that mistakes, however humiliating, were okay; I would have felt like I'd disgraced myself, my school, and tainted the long, esteemed history of the Rosell name. I'd have thought that I'd made my classmates ashamed, like they were Nobel Laureates and I was an imbecile who had stumbled into their midst. I would have told myself: *See! Told you you were going to screw this up! Good going, Roy!* Worst of all, I would have fallen more deeply under fear's control.

But on this occasion, I didn't allow fear, doubt, or panic to dictate my reaction. I didn't cower or try to erase the memory of that horrific embarrassment, and I didn't beat myself up over it. I accepted what had occurred, calmed myself, and treated the situation for what it was: another bump in the road to controlling my fear. I asked my professor and some classmates what they thought I could do to improve. I analyzed what went wrong, took the feedback, and developed a list of ways I could better myself for the next speech. What I came up with was this:

Don't say dumb things: I was in an upper division marketing class asking them if they knew what the 4 P's of Marketing were (a basic marketing concept), and there was no clever or cool reason for me to ask that question. *Lesson learned: The audience is smart. No need to dumb down the presentation.*

Don't pre-plan conversations: There's no issue with planning questions to ask the audience, but their reaction and follow-up questions and commentary should be natural. Though my presentation was meant to be conversational and I tried hard to do just that, it was forced. So, the audience felt awkward responding to my inquiries. *Lesson learned: Not everything needs to be planned. Leave enough room for genuine interaction and spontaneity.*

Have fun: Just because a topic isn't one I'd normally perceive as exciting, that doesn't mean I have to give a serious, research-driven talk. I'm presenting to human beings. Human beings, by nature, want to have a good time. *Lesson learned: Make creating a fun presentation a priority.*

Be funny: I'm normally a funny guy, but I stripped all the humor out of my presentation. As a result, I stripped the audience of their opportunity to laugh. *Lesson learned: A little humor won't kill anyone. But having no humor could kill your presentation.*

Dress your research in party clothes: Though my intro may have suggested the opposite, my presentation had a ton of great information in it. Graphs, charts, interesting data…but none of it hit home with the audience because the way I presented wasn't interesting. As a result, all that awesome research went to waste. It's like singing a song with the best lyrics ever written, but singing it out-of-tune. *Lesson learned: Sometimes numbers and data fly over people's heads. Present it in a memorable way so it sticks.*

The next time I was set to give a presentation, I pulled out the document I'd made those notes on and checked off each item one by one, just to make sure I wouldn't make any of those mistakes again. Since then, I've always made it a priority to ask members of the audience after my speech what they thought I could have done better. I've learned that there is always room for improvement and that by and large, audiences are supportive and are cheering you on.

But listen, that's not to say that leaving glossophobia behind is easy peasy. It's not. Sometimes, you take one step forward and five steps back. Sometimes, just when you think you're on the verge of a breakthrough, life puts a big, clunky roadblock in your path to test your resilience. So here's my advice: Expect this so you're not caught off guard if it happens.

If everything seems to be going down the toilet, know that you're not presenting to vultures just waiting for a gaffe. The audience is hoping to take something valuable away from your speech, so don't be so hard on yourself. Instead, analyze what went wrong. The way I reacted to my "4 P's" debacle is how you should react to screw-ups: accept them, analyze what went wrong, then take every lesson you can to better yourself. Most importantly, give it another shot as soon as you can.

We glossophobes are so concerned with what everyone is thinking about us that we sacrifice the opportunity to grow and mature. For me, treating each failure as a valuable lesson and being aware of (and totally okay with) the possibility of screwing up was the second step to becoming the person I had always striven to be onstage.

But, this is easier said than done. Recovering from a self-defined speaking catastrophe like the one I faced above was not easy. I was humiliated, my self-esteem took a hit, and I wasn't entirely sure if I wanted to give a speech ever again in my life. Fortunately, I realized that I couldn't let it get me down, because that would only make future presentations worse.

This wasn't my first public speaking disaster, and I didn't always react so positively to them as I had done in the 4 P's debacle. In my freshman year of high school, for example, I faced a speaking catastrophe so daunting that it completely drained me, and I didn't recover for several years. At the time, I couldn't figure out what I had done wrong, and why I kept messing up. In hindsight, I know exactly what I could have done better. I'll tell you the story in the next chapter, so you can learn from my blunders.

Risk This #10: Gather constructive feedback

After your next speech, ask three people what you could have done to make it a more valuable experience for them. Summarize their feedback, then pick three recommendations you will implement in your next speeches. If you don't have a speech coming up, make your own opportunity—offer to present on a current event topic, give a toast at a dinner, present research findings, or volunteer to speak up at a school, work, or a community event.

CHAPTER 12:

Recovering From Speaking Catastrophes – A Message to Terrible Speakers

A CEO was scheduled to speak at an important convention, so he asked his assistant to write him a tight, twenty-minute speech. When the CEO returned from the big event, he was furious. "What's the idea of writing me an hour-long speech?" he demanded. "Half the audience walked out before I finished." Baffled, his assistant responded, "I wrote you a twenty-minute speech. I also gave you the two extra copies you asked for."

—Anonymous

S ome of the speeches I've conducted in my life have been nothing short of preposterous. I've forgotten my script in its entirety moments before presenting. I've farted on stage. I've been monotonous, incoherent, put half a dozen people to sleep, and once gave an entire presentation with my zipper down.

If you had asked me a few years ago how I could be so dreadful at speechifying, I'd shrug and say something like: "I don't know, man…giving speeches just isn't for me. I've tried everything the experts suggest but nothing seems to work...."

Even though I'd tell everyone, including myself, that I just wasn't built to give good speeches, I knew full well that the terrible presentations were not a result of a pre-existing inability. I sucked at giving speeches because I subconsciously made the decision to suck at giving speeches. I didn't want to suck, but I wasn't willing to put in the work and go through the initial discomfort to not suck.

One of my most nightmarish public speaking experiences happened in the first semester of my freshman year in high school. I wanted to take a computer class as an elective, but my parents had forced me to sign up for speech class. Mom said it would help with my confidence and help me get over my abhorrence of being on stage. Dad said maybe it'd make me grow some cojones. I wanted cojones, so I stepped up.

Gabrielino High School

Freshman year speech class

Our first assignment was to find a partner in class and spend three weeks memorizing and practicing a scene from a movie or book. Thankfully, my only friend in high school at the time, Tom, was in class with me, so we teamed up. We decided to go with Dr. Seuss's *Hooray for Diffendoofer Day!*

At first, we formed a glorious partnership—we locked ourselves in the practice room and rehearsed like madmen, having the time of our lives. But as presentation day crept closer, the magnitude of the task began to infect our positivity. *We're about to act out a Dr. Seuss book in front of our peers, in the first weeks of high school, where we're already having a hard time making friends.* One day before our performance, Tom cracked under the pressure and dropped out of class.

I informed the teacher that we wouldn't be able to do the performance anymore because I no longer had a partner. He shot back with, "Lucky you, now you don't have to worry about sharing the spotlight!"

The next day was presentation day. After the first few speeches, the teacher announced, "Up next isssssssss…."

My body stiffened. I kept my hands on my desktop, my eyes fixed on the front of the classroom. I held my breath. A cold sensation came over me. My only movement was my cold, sweat-drenched hands, slowly gliding across the desk. With each second that passed, the pressure in my stomach intensified.

He scanned the room with a devilish smile—a smile so terrifyingly devious that I remember it perfectly almost fifteen years later. He sought his next victim for what felt like an eternity, looking each student square in the eyes. Our eyes locked. His lips spread and the corners of his mouth curved upward, forming a big, creepy, Grinch-like smile.

"Roy Rosell presenting *Hooray for Diffendoofer Day!* Everyone, let's give Roy a HOORAY on his big DAY!"

I stood up. The short-lived applause and obligatory "hoorays" ceased and all I could hear were my footsteps. I was quickly losing the sensation in my face. I felt my classmate's eyes burning holes in my back.

I got to center stage, turned to the class. *Should I say hello? Introduce myself? Introduce my speech? Small talk? Ask them something? Just start?* I elected to wave at them. No one waved back. This sent a sharp jolt down my spine. I put my hand in my pocket and quickly took it out. A piece of lint went floating to the floor. I thought of my dying reputation and quickly scratched my neck, then my knee, then picked at a pimple on my chin. I thought of my social image and wiped the sweat off my temple, then itched the back of my ear. I thought of dealing with years of being bullied for what was about to occur.

I began. "I've always lived in Dinkerville, my friends all live here too...." My knees started to tremble, and my voice cracked. I looked up, briefly, in hopes of seeing the wide-eyed, attentive, and supportive faces of my classmates. What I saw instead was a collection of half-asleep, bored, and disinterested faces staring back at me.

"We go to Diffendoofer School, and we're happy that we do...." My throat closed, I lost my breath.

"Our school is at the corner of Dinkzoober and Dinkzott...." Tears formed in the corners of my eyes.

"It looks like any other school, but...." I heard a loud ringing in my ears.

"But...." The pressure in my stomach deepened, shooting a gust of frigid air into my chest.

"But...."

I stood, silent. I concentrated on avoiding an explosion of tears. Then, it hit me. I had forgotten my lines. The same lines I had rehearsed hundreds of times in that practice room. The same lines I could easily have recited to myself or my family time and time again without a single hiccup.

I stood there, no notes to fall back on. I looked up at the class, desperation in my eyes. They stared like a mob of thirsty vampires who had stumbled upon a blood drive. After about ten more seconds, with nothing to say, on the verge of a nervous breakdown; the teacher finally ended my misery. "Thanks Roy! Let's give Roy a big HOORAY! We'll try this again tomorrow!"

This nightmarish experience repeated itself for another six class sessions. I presented every day, getting a little further each time, dying a little more inside with each unbroken silence. On the sixth day, I dropped out of speech class. On the seventh day, I left that class of full-bellied, satisfied vampires, and rested in computer class.

I gave up. I didn't want to put myself in that vulnerable situation ever again, but I knew I had to minimize my fear to a level that didn't terrorize my existence. I wanted to sit in a therapy session for an hour and be cured. I wanted it to be easy, and if I wasn't going to get 'easy,' I'd wait for another opportunity.

I never wanted to feel that embarrassment again, so after that class, I stopped making myself vulnerable. From then on, I'd type out the full speech and instead of interacting with my audience, I'd read straight off the paper. If there were wording issues in the paper I was reading, I'd read through them like Anchorman Ron Burgundy when they changed the contents of his teleprompter.

That *Diffendoofer Day* presentation was the first of many I'd be required to conduct in my first couple of years in high school. Just when I thought I'd escaped having to give speeches, I'd looked at the syllabus of each of my classes and saw them riddled with mandatory presentations. And after two years, I wasn't happy with the way my presentations were going.

With each dreadful speech, I dug a deeper hole for myself. Instead of concentrating my efforts on improving upon each underwhelming presentation, I elected to keep doing the same thing over and over again, to avoid further embarrassment. I didn't trust that I was capable of giving a great speech—and I didn't want to put in a ton of work and risk humiliation for a reward that wasn't guaranteed. That decision kept me locked in fear's grasp for a long time. The lingering thought in my mind throughout high school became: "I'm a terrible speaker, how could I not be scared?"

Taming Fear Through Effective Preparation

Today, I realize that people are terrible at things because they haven't put in the extra effort to get good at them. I don't mean that they don't want it badly enough, don't spend enough time working on it, or that they don't put in the effort. I mean they don't prepare effectively. *Effective preparation, Roy—that's the key!* People (my past self included) sometimes think that "being prepared" means mastering a subject, or memorizing a presentation. Well, I'd recited *Diffendoofer Day* to myself in a practice room many times without a single hiccup. Isn't that proper preparation? Yet I'd choke within the first minute of being on stage, every time.

Before presenting *Diffendoofer Day,* I'd assumed that because I performed it successfully on my own, I should have been able to do it in front of a classroom. After all, I'd been taught that mastery comes through the amount of time you put in to something. *Well, if that's the case,* I thought, *I should have blown the audience away with 'Diffendoofer Day.'* But I'd prepared, and I hadn't nailed it. I was a lost cause. I'd crumbled repeatedly. I couldn't take it anymore—so as I noted, I dropped out of class.

But what I realized later is that I'd prepared but I hadn't prepared *effectively.* Effective preparation considers that practicing in front of a mirror and presenting to an audience are two different beasts. On your own, you concentrate on yourself: your tone, your movement, your knowledge of the topic. These are important factors to work on prior to your speech, but they aren't the only factors. When you're in front of an audience, your nervousness, the audience's attention span, their piercing eyes, and their perceived expectations become center focus. As a result, that "mastery" of your topic becomes obsolete, putting you at risk of fumbling, forgetting, even momentarily losing your basic motor skills during your presentation.

Ask yourself: "Have I prepared for the possibility that I'll lose my place in my talk?" "What if I realize the audience isn't as interested as I thought they'd be?" "What if I have a presentation malfunction?" The answers to these questions are essential to effective preparation.

When practicing for my *Diffendoofer Day* performance, I didn't consider that maybe the audience wouldn't have as much fun watching me as I thought they would. So, I didn't prepare myself mentally for their potential disinterest and I didn't plan anything to get them more involved. As a result, I was completely thrown off when I saw their disinterested faces and couldn't recover. I didn't prepare for the possibility that I'd forget my lines either, so I didn't have notecards, visual cues, or anything else up my sleeve to get me back on track. Worst of all, I didn't even bother trying to redefine my nervousness. Instead, it crushed me.

With that speech, I failed. And after each of my seven *Diffendoofer Day* failures, I went home and tried to memorize my speech even more. It didn't occur to me that it wasn't my memorization that needed work—I had that part down. What I needed was to be prepared—for losing my place, for losing the audience's attention, for losing my sanity. I left all of that up in the air, trusting I'd just figure things out as they happened. Because of that, things didn't go the way they could have. If I had realized that back then and had made sure I'd prepared for my presentations *effectively*, I may have overcome my glossophobia in the ninth grade.

A big part of the reason I gave up that time (and countless other times (in different ways) between the ages of ten and twenty-three) was because I hadn't made a Pact with myself—an unbreakable promise that, no matter what difficulties I faced, I wouldn't do myself that damaging disservice of giving up. Let me tell you about that next.

Risk This #11: Screwing up

Prepare a presentation with slides, then set up a camera (a phone camera leaned up against a wall is fine) and film yourself presenting it. When you watch the footage, do the following:

Note what you do when you lose your place, get uncomfortable, or forget what the next part of your presentation is.

If it looks awkward, list ways you could make getting back on track look seamless.

CHAPTER 13:

Burning the Bridge to Complacency – Making the Pact

"From this moment on, I hereby promise myself that I will do whatever is necessary, however difficult or nerve-wracking, to overcome my fear. I will not stop, take a break, or give myself any leniency until I've achieved this goal."

— Roy Rosell strikes again.

In the three months before my commencement speech, I approached my battle with fear with the same set of tools I'd always had. I was still the same tall, goofy, awkward guy with a big afro and sweaty hands. I still had butterflies in my stomach, a tremble in my voice, and an uncanny ability to forget everything I was supposed to say at critical moments. I was still willing to work hard, too. Technically, I did get a little better at presenting, but my improvement as a speaker did not warrant going from panicking in front of a class of twenty students throughout college, to feeling excited about a presentation in front of 15,000. But that's exactly what happened. It wasn't luck, Voodoo, or a mystical event—neither was it a revamp of my approach. It was a mental shift. I adopted the belief that this time, I wasn't going to back down. This time, I would be victorious.

After my commencement speech, when I finally had the mental freedom from fear, I started watching speakers with a more analytical eye and discovered that even those who look comfortable are feeling the wrath of glossophobia. After almost every speech, I asked presenters who'd performed well whether they were nervous during their presentations. The typical responses I'd get were, "You could tell?" and "I was about to pass out up there!"

Aside from a couple of special cases, almost no one told me they weren't nervous to some extent. Even successful presenters who were petrified covered their fear well. Next time you're on stage thinking you're the only one feeling nervous, remember: stop wasting your time trying to hide your anxiety. Just accept it. You're nervous, and that's fine. Focus on giving a presentation the audience will enjoy, not on how your stomach feels. Focusing on the audience's enjoyment will bring a whole new realm of possibilities for you to excel in onstage. It will make you look confident—and when you look confident, people want to listen. From there, it's a chain reaction of wonderful things.

For that mental shift to occur for me, there were four things I needed to realize and do (the fourth being the most important). Once I did these four things, my mental outlook changed. Whereas before I'd felt like a tuna fish flopping on a fisherman's deck, awaiting my ginger-and-wasabi-paired fate; now I saw the opportunity to present as a chance to chip away at my fear. I didn't see the stage as my enemy. I saw it as my ultimate challenge, one I knew I'd conquer. Here's the four things I did that helped me to stop worrying about *me*, and start focusing on *them*:

1. I realized that I never look as bad as I feel

When I was at my worst with glossophobia, I felt alone as I watched everyone present as if they were mini Poseidons, speaking to the fish of the sea. But later, I discovered that people couldn't tell that my stomach was eating itself from the inside out or that I'd been contemplating jumping out the window for days.

For most of my life, I would have taken any form of torture in place of giving a speech. I agonized for years, fighting every day to gain control of my collapsing confidence—and, more often than not, failing miserably. But when I finally revealed my level of terror to people who watched me present, no one could believe I was nervous. They didn't notice my trembling hands, the way my throat started to close, or my desperate panic, and they didn't know that the smile pasted on my face was there to cover the fact that everything was not fine and dandy.

2. I figured out where my fear comes from

There's a group you can blame for your fear of public speaking: wimpy cavemen. The design of the human brain—given that it's been around for hundreds of thousands of years longer than public speaking—makes it extremely difficult to stop fearing what it knows is the worst tactical position to be in. The "worst tactical position" is standing alone, in an open space, with nowhere to hide, without a weapon, facing a large group of creatures staring at you. Sounds familiar, doesn't it? Here's how it all began:

Scenario 1: Mr. Fearless-Caveman takes a stroll in the wilderness. A vicious thunderstorm approaches. He decides to seek shelter and rushes into the nearest cave. Once inside, he realizes he's not alone—there's a big bear in that cave! So, Mr. Fearless-Caveman kicks back his feet, lowers his head, and gets ready to attack the hungry cave bear with his sharp antlers. But wait...he has no antlers. Let's start over....

Scenario 2: Mr. Fearless-Caveman looks the angry bear in the eyes, opens wide to expose his poisonous fangs, and gets ready to spray skin-melting acid from his razor sharp...hold on a sec...no fangs or poisonous acid? Okay... try again.

Scenario 3: Mr. Fearless-Caveman sees the cave bear, takes a deep breath and resorts to his shell where he will be safe from the frustrated bear until he finally gives up and leaves him alone...huh? He didn't have a shell, either?

None of these scenarios occurred—what really happened was that Mr. Fearless-Caveman was torn to a million pieces, his DNA forever lost in the cave's soil and a satisfied cave bear walked out, belly filled with enough protein to last him a month.

Eventually, hunter-gatherers stopped entering these caves, wherein they (rightfully) anticipated horrors beyond measure. And, even if they needed to go into the cave for protection from the elements, they couldn't—they would have preferred to suffer or roam endlessly to find another sanctuary than go into that cave. The following generation of hunter-gatherers did the same. It didn't matter that the threat of the cave bear didn't exist anymore—they had upgraded their weapons and travelled in groups—because the fear of caves was instilled in them.

We are the great, great (x1000's) grandchildren of those cave-fearing hunter-gatherers. And the podium is the great, great (x1000's) grandchild of that scary cave. Except bear caves aren't podiums and Neanderthal-world-daily-reality-threats, like onslaughts of saber-toothed tigers, swarms of locusts, or assaults by giant prehistoric flesh-eating birds just aren't realistic anymore.

So, I'm about to reveal the one thing glossophobes crave to hear: "You're not to blame for your fear of public speaking." Genetically speaking, it's natural for you to fear public speaking. And it sucks that we must suffer today for the actions of our wimpy ancestors. But while it's not our fault, here's some great news: We all have the power to do something about it. The task of overcoming fear is 100 percent in our control. But in order to progress, we must stop blaming genetics, social anxiety, speech disorders, or whatever excuses we can generate. The justifications serve only to put a big, fat roadblock in our path forward. If you keep sharing control of your fate, you'll remain powerless in your battle.

Fear of public speaking is your default setting. But as with anything else, default settings can and should be altered to create the best version of you.

3. *I made fear my best friend*

I use the words "kill" and "overcome" when referring to fear. I don't mean this in the literal sense, obviously. Your goal should never be to eliminate fear from your life—that would be counterproductive. Fear is what makes you likeable, shows you care, and makes you human. Whether it's pursuing musical stardom, launching an entrepreneurial venture, or writing a book (wink wink)—anything worth doing requires that you partner up with fear first. Fear is the signal that you're on the right path to achieving greatness. This is because anything that makes you better has an imaginary contractual agreement attached to it. That agreement has a clause in it that states:

If you undertake this [enter activity/decision/journey here], there's a chance you may temporarily experience one or more of the following:

- Failure
- Rejection
- Disappointment
- Embarrassment
- Grief
- Anxiety
- Isolation
- A drop in confidence
- Damaged ego
- Depression
- Panic
- Hopelessness.

The thought that your decision may temporarily result in one or more of those emotional ramifications is what keeps us from doing the things that make life worth living. It's the fear of these consequences that makes us hesitate, reconsider, and ultimately, make decisions that stunt our progress. Remember, Fear = Care = Motivation for Success.

4. I made an unbreakable pact with myself

What triggered the mindset required to control my fear wasn't anything out of the ordinary. It wasn't yoga that made me forget my worries or a hypnosis-induced trance that made me a new man. The thing that got me to overcome my fear of public speaking was belief and the unbreakable pact I made with myself.

THE PACT

From this moment on, I hereby promise myself that I will do whatever necessary, however difficult or nerve-wracking, to overcome my fear. I will not stop, take a break or give myself any leniency until I've achieved this goal. I will not make excuses and even though I know this will be challenging, and I will feel like quitting, I will not give up. Nothing can and nothing will stop me now.

Keep in mind, getting your fear to a level that more closely resembles excitement than nervousness, like the feeling a thrill-seeker gets when waiting in line for a roller coaster, is dependent on whether or not you are willing to do what it takes to succeed. It's not committing to a workout plan, then quitting on Day 3. It's not starting a book and abandoning the project fifty pages in. It's saying, "This is what I want to achieve, this is what I'm going to do to achieve it, and I'm not stopping until I've accomplished my goal." So often, we make a decision to do what is necessary to reach our goals when in reality we've just signed up to try until it gets too uncomfortable.

Once I made *The Pact* with myself, a lot of things changed. As much as certain situations terrified me, hesitation, overwhelming fear, and Doubt were no longer hindrances. Instead, they became signals to take action. Every time I saw an opportunity to do something that freaked the bejesus out of me, and I'd feel that sinking feeling in my stomach, I'd use that feeling to motivate me to just jump and get it over with.

It was this positive reaction to hesitation, fear, and Doubt that got me my first job out of college (and every job thereafter), allowed me to build my professional network, rekindle old friendships, and create new opportunities for myself. It's masochistic in a sense—you must strive to do things that are painful. You must do the things that make your heart race. You must act when fear starts to carve through your insides.

If overcoming your fear is worth the struggle, then sign *The Pact* with blood (not literally, of course). Know that, though the fear of public speaking may appear to be a monster now, you have the power to make fear work for you.

Once you've done that, it's time to learn how to actually *stick* to the Pact. We can all throw around promises like hotcakes, but the tough part is sticking to them. That part is achieved through positivity. You're probably thinking: God damn it, Roy. Here I was expecting some shocking revelation, but instead you throw this generic positivity crap at me. I'm over this book." And to that I say, *I know*. It sounds super lame. I hate hearing the "be positive" stuff too. But in the coming chapters, I'll explain *why you should care.*

Risk This #12: Remember "The Pact"

Write down *The Pact* on a notecard. Put it in your wallet or purse. Frame it and put it up on your bedroom wall or office desk. Set it up on your phone as a daily reminder. Keep it with you at all times and, whenever you feel yourself doubt your ability or start to cower at the mere idea of a speaking opportunity, pull out *The Pact* and read it aloud three times.

PART 3

THE ELUSIVE PHENOMENON OF POSITIVE THINKING – AND HOW TO MASTER IT

CHAPTER 14:

Positive Thinking = Success?
Get Outa Here!

*"There is always going to be someone smarter than you, someone with
more knowledge, with better work experience, with a more prestigious
educational background. But, regardless of other factors, know that there is
not a single person on this planet that will work harder than you."*

—ME, from my commencement speech again.
Throwing out that motivational fire.

Before making the Pact, bailing on my goals was easy peasy. When
things got tough, I could come up with myriad justifications to
convince myself that giving up was okay. I mastered the craft
of excuse-making and as a result, I seldom accomplished anything
noteworthy. A prime example of this was my endless struggle to stick to
a workout routine without quitting when my schedule changed or I lost
motivation. My most noteworthy attempt at this was about a year before
graduating from college.

I realized I was unable to run a block without collapsing in a puddle of sweat. So, I decided it was time to get in shape. I cut junk food from my diet, started a rigorous morning exercise routine, and told myself I'd stick with it. I did—until I took a trip with my buddies and the temptation of all-you-can-eat greasy foreign cuisine became too tempting. So, I abandoned my diet and ramped up the intensity at the gym to make up for it. Then winter came. It got chilly. I had an early class so getting out of my warm bed at 5:30 a.m. to work out sounded as enticing as taking an ice bath.

I started going to the gym after school instead. At that hour, the gym was crowded—people left weights all over the damn place, and I didn't have the patience to find the ones I needed. I also had to deal with sweaty bodybuilders waiting impatiently for me to finish my sets on the bench press. On top of that, all I could think about at the gym was the homework I had to do. Frustration overcame me.

So, I stopped going to the gym after school and elected instead to double my workouts on weekends and "whenever I can fit it into my schedule." After a few weeks, I realized that working out on weekends was not nearly enough to get in shape and "whenever I can fit it in" became "never"—surprise! So, I figured my time would be better spent doing something that would glean better results. But I was jumping from class to class, plagued with endless piles of homework, and sticking to a strict diet was inconvenient. Within a couple of months, I'd dropped the diet, dumped the workout plan, lost my motivation to get in shape—and picked up a family-size bag of Doritos.

I gave up. Though I'd made *The Pact* with myself, and thought I was motivated, the reality was I was only willing to fight until the battle got too difficult. I'd subconsciously convinced myself that the sacrifices, the cold mornings, and the countless delicious meals I'd had to give up to achieve my goal were not worth it. I decided to consult with my father.

Me: "Papa, tengo una pregunta (I have a question). Why can't I stick to my workout plan? I want to get in shape more than anything, but I keep giving up...."

Papa: *Bolts to his room to recover photos from his bodybuilding days after the Vietnam war.** "Roycito. Mira (look). Look at these photos. Mira my chest. Do you think I got like this giving up? Look at this one. Mira esta figura (look at this figure)! Do you think eight-pack abs happen to someone with a wimpy-limpy mind?"

Me: "But Dad, I want to be buff. It's so hard to find the time. I have classes from 7:00 a.m. to 5:00 p.m., work from...."

Papa: "Oh! *Que pena, hijo* (what a shame, son). I'm so sorry you're too busy. President Obama can fit a workout into his daily schedule. Vladimir Putin can fit a workout into his schedule. But *mi hijo Roycito*, college student who doesn't have to worry about bills, gets his *comida* cooked by his mama, drives a car his papa bought him—doesn't have time to work out."

Me: "But, I just have so much...."

Papa: "Wake up, hijo! *Cortala (cut it out)*! Stop being so negative. You will never achieve what you set your mind to if you're not positive!"

Be positive? Did my tough-as-nails, war hero father just quote one of those wimpy-limpy self-help phrases? What do I need positivity for? I need more hours in the day, less homework—not more positivity.... Little did I know at the time, my schedule would only get more packed, my responsibilities would only grow, and my free time would only diminish.

Today, I look back at that time of my life, and I realize that it was positivity and a focus on the finish line that kept me going those first few weeks. I genuinely believed I would reach the finish line and I was willing to endure the sacrifices needed to get there. Opening the door for doubt is what caused it all to start crumbling down. I didn't drop my goal to get in shape because my schedule got too busy. I stopped because my doubt convinced me it wasn't worth the struggle. Papa was right!

Do You Need Positive Thinking to Achieve Success?

About halfway through writing this book, I got into an online skirmish about the power of positivity with an older gentleman who runs a public speaking assistance program in the U.K. He'd read an article I'd written about how positive thinking and the rejection of doubt transformed my life. He insisted I was mistaken—that I was just confused. He argued: "How much positivity do you need to ride a bicycle—or, once you've learned (and you keep learning), do you just get on with it? Once you know you can do something effectively, you don't need to make a big deal of it in your thinking."

He raised an interesting argument: Do you *need* positive thinking to achieve success? Can pessimists become top-level executives, successful athletes, and great public speakers? In my experience with public speaking, working out, entrepreneurial ventures, or anything I've tried and failed at, it was always the things I believed I would achieve that ended with the results I wanted. But after some inconclusive research, I decided to gather more data.

So, I applied to be an event host at the largest gathering of business leaders in America. Everyone from top executives at Google and Facebook to Paramount Pictures, Red Bull, and ESPN gathered to brainstorm the next generation of products, network with each other and party. I visualized that I'd get a call from the recruiter, blow their minds in the interview, and make it impossible for them to reject me. All of that happened. But was my positive thinking the reason?

As an aspiring marketer, surrounded by hundreds of business leaders and the most creative minds of the twenty-first century, I felt like a fat little kid at Hometown Buffet. I pranced around, picking brains, trying to figure out the association between these executives' successes and positive thinking.

Ninety percent of the leaders I talked to spoke about success philosophically—about the power of visualization, relentless positivity, and having an unshakeable belief that "I'll achieve what I dream of achieving." They spoke of "setting your goals, working hard, and trusting the process." They didn't mention degrees, training, or professional development.

Then there was the ten percent who told it straight. They talked about taking emotions out of work, that there are no "friends" in business, and suggested I form a long list of business connections to support my climb to triumph. They talked about a relentless work ethic, being the first in and last out, meditating to stay sane, and fighting to the death for what I want—no mention of having an A+ attitude.

To the few that gave me the latter responses, I asked an additional question: "I'm a pessimist. I'm going to work my butt off, but I'm not sure my efforts will result in me achieving my goal. Can I kill my fears and rise through the ranks with a negative attitude?"

This caught them off-guard. Some laughed and diverted the question. Others gave me a straightforward "No!" Some stumbled and fumbled to avoid putting me out of my misery— "Well, if you work extra hard, I guess you can achieve most things." The general response to the revelation of my pessimism was, well, pessimistic.

I dug further about the consistent affirmations of these successful individuals. I wanted to know what it was about positive thinking that helped them to achieve monumental success, and I wanted to hear more than that "positivity attracts good things" and that "the universe rewards positivity." I had read about all that. What I gathered from them was surprisingly enlightening. Following are the *Benefits of Positivity*, summarized by some of the most successful people in the world:

1. You'll recognize opportunities with far more clarity

Negativity clouds your ability to identify potential opportunities and the paths necessary to harness them. You may still *see* opportunities but with a negative outlook, you'll convince yourself that the opportunity isn't attainable or worth it, and more often than not, you'll let it pass. Positivity will open the doors for you to design a clear blueprint for maximizing those opportunities and will instill in you a belief that you can realize your goals.

2. You'll exude confidence

With a high level of confidence, you'll be more capable of tackling the same challenges that your negative self would have brushed aside as being too hard or "not worth it." Projecting an air of confidence will also make people perceive you as more capable and trustworthy.

3. You'll get more creative

When you turn your concentration from negative to positive, you'll be free to focus your efforts on designing innovative solutions for achieving your goals. When you're down, the idea-generating part of your brain is busy thinking about how to make the situation at hand less terrible, thus limiting your ability to be creative.

4. You'll bring more success to your life

When you're feeling good, you'll strive to bring more of that good into your life. When you expect success, that expectation stimulates in you the will to continue to attain more success. When positive desire is mixed with the ability to recognize opportunities and the confidence to tackle any challenges, that's one ass-kicking, success-producing combo.

5. You'll be heads up above the competition

There will always be people with more experience, a more expansive set of skills, and a more prestigious educational background than you. Often, you'll be competing directly with these people for opportunities. Having a positive attitude can give you an incredible advantage. Positivity has the potential of covering for any deficiencies you might have in background or experience, allowing you to beat out people who are better qualified.

When I realized what these successful individuals were doing, everything started to make more sense. But even with this newly acquired knowledge, I still had my reservations. I had reservations because one of my best friends is an optimist, and he's barely able to pay his rent. And I've never heard my cousin say a negative thing about himself, but he's been stuck with the same terrible job for the past five years. Another good friend has fixated his vision on a career in entertainment, stays hyper-focused on his goal, but the closest he's gotten is mopping the floors at a movie theater.

I used to question why some people succeed and others who work just as hard spend their lives at the bottom. *Why,* I asked myself, *does the guy who didn't put in an ounce of effort manage to get so good at public speaking, while other people work their butts off, and still feel and sound like hyperventilating donkeys?* And expanding on that thought, *Why are there countless examples of people working their butts off to achieve a goal, yet only a select few make it?* I wanted to stop feeling resentment towards the people who were doing better than me. Hee-haw.

Risk This #13: Quitting too soon

Write down an example of a time you were motivated to accomplish something (getting in shape, writing a book, etc.), started it, but gave up too soon. Then jot down notes for the following questions:

- Why did you give up?
- What would you do differently if you had the opportunity to redo it now?

Once you've done this exercise, pick something you want to accomplish (if still applicable, the same thing you gave up on before), put together an action plan, and get to work to make it happen.

CHAPTER 15:

Why We Try So Hard, Why We Give Up – And How to Break the Trend

"Start now—with your current set of circumstances, with all your pain, fear, doubt, and uncertainty. Don't wait for another day. Start now, work hard, and trust the process. It takes this level of courage to achieve your dreams."

—ME, after finally *acting* instead of *analyzing*,

and realizing the glorious consequences

As I write this chapter, I feel a lingering fear that someday, I'll lose the drive to finish this book. Either that, or, the countless hours I'll spend will result in nothing more than a few copies passed out to my family and friends. I'll have to bear the awkward, "Oh, Roycito, good yob on your book, I lob et!" and, "Ah que pena, por qué no lo escribiste en Español (What a shame, why didn't you write it in Spanish)?" from my relatives, and the odd "Way to go, pal!" from friends. There is also the possibility that I'll finish this book, completely miscalculate the demand for it, and end up so deeply in debt that I'll be praying for a Communist takeover—from the book fort I've built in a downtown Los Angeles freeway underpass. I've got a prime location picked out.

Losing motivation sucks. I remember more than a dozen occasions where my motivation crumbled—the resulting regret from not following through has stuck with me. I've been wildly motivated to accomplish the goals I set for myself, only to find that the pursuit of them has been rife with challenges, internal battles, and the ever-present question: "Is this worth the struggle?" It has happened when attempting to advance my career, trying to become a professional soccer player, and for most of my life, with struggling to overcome my fear of public speaking.

With my entertainment career, for example, I knew I had to network like a madman to move up in the industry. I was young and motivated, working in Music at Fox Sports, and decided I'd set up lunches with all the executives I'd been stalking on LinkedIn. But it didn't take long for me to realize that building connections wasn't easy. I'd have to deal with constant rejection, craft personalized emails, and make time at the end of work to write to all of these people. A couple of months later, I gave up. After more than two years, no promotion in sight, I lost hope and left the entertainment business altogether.

With soccer, I had dreamed of becoming a professional goalkeeper. I trained hard during college, got myself a personal trainer, and remained freakishly motivated. But when I joined a team where I had to be a backup to someone better than me, my pride was crushed and my motivation took a hit. I decided I wasn't made to be a pro athlete, so I gave that up too.

With the fear of public speaking, I gave up a bunch of times, but unlike my other goals, I kept coming back to try again. I knew I had to control my fear, but I kept postponing it. Each time I unleashed my forces on my fear, I hit a point where I asked myself: "This is really hard…is it actually going to work?" Each time, I'd convince myself that it wouldn't.

The belief I held that I'd fall short no matter how hard I tried kept my efforts subdued. Instead of pushing through when I saw the smooth road rising at the end of each pothole-ridden path I was walking on, I would sit down and wait for Caltrans to come and fix it. While I was waiting, I'd strategize endlessly on ways to make sure my efforts would be fail-proof. It shouldn't have taken half my life to get over my fear. At the end of college, in those all-important three months, I finally realized that there's only one way to assure success: work hard, learn from your failures, and don't stop until you've achieved what you set your mind to. How resilient you are will dictate how much you achieve.

Whether it's pursuing entrepreneurial success, mastering a language, or doing anything that requires time, perseverance, and unyielding dedication to achieve; many people wait until…well, they just keep on waiting. The reason for this procrastination is that they are waiting until they have more time, less responsibility, more money, better technology, less risk, until the damn stars align. But that perfect moment will never arrive. Next time you're thinking you're ready to give it your all, remember:

Start now—with your current set of circumstances, with all your pain, fear, doubt, and uncertainty. Don't wait for another day. Start now, work hard and trust the process. It takes this level of courage to achieve your dreams.

Before I made the decision to start and not to stop until I had succeeded in banishing fear, my head wasn't screwed on straight. I avoided all the things that would make me overcome my fear, electing instead to fill that time with inconsequential matters, scraping by on the lazy man's definition of effort ("I'll try if it's easy!"). I gasped and grumbled as fear failed to move an inch.

Silencing the Negative Influencers

Something else that holds us back from achievement is negative influencers. Unless you have the mental fortitude of a serial killer, the comments, opinions, and suggestions of others will probably influence you. The first influencer that characterized my battle with fear is the one some people call "haters." Record producer DJ Khaled refers to them as "THEY." Though there are outside factors characterized by this definition, most of the time, this influencer is yourself—after all, as a glossophobe, you are the only person holding yourself back. Other times, you'll come across someone just like you, who'll hear of your mission, progress, and goals, and they'll plant a seed of doubt to derail you.

The second influencer is God's Chosen Child. These people claim to have had the same problems as you, but have found the miraculous solution in something you've already tried. During my struggle, I've heard many ambitious statements, but there's one that I read in the tenth year of my struggle that really had me questioning whether I was capable of winning: "Fear of public speaking has been an enormous thorn in my side my entire adult life. I always knew I was basically well-adjusted, give or take a quirk or two, but, because of this seemingly insurmountable interior obstacle, this hidden limitation I told myself I couldn't get over, a small part of me clung to the idea that there might be something seriously wrong with me."

Yes...YES! I know exactly what you're talking about bud! Thank goodness, I'm not alone!

"...Then I read a sensational self-help book and attended the author's weekend workshop. My experience of the workshop: It was like being wheeled in wearing a body cast Saturday morning and walking out on my own two feet, with only a slight limp, Sunday evening!"

Really? Because I've read that book and did most of the things the workshop itinerary said to do and I still feel like Courage the Cowardly Dog every time I get up to speak.

"If you feel like you're going to die at the thought of public speaking, get this book, go to the workshop and choose a new way to live instead."

So, there I was, with a decade of battling this fear under my belt, and God's Chosen Child reads a book, goes to a workshop, and is completely cured. Of course, my first reaction was: *Phenomenal, oh lord of self-healing. Bestow your supreme wisdom upon our undeserving souls! Lead us peasants to our inner lion!* While I now understand that these people have good intentions, back then my bitterness consumed me and I felt hopeless.

Why were things that had no effect on me changing the lives of others? What was I missing? Well, I learned that you can shed blood, sweat, and tears to overcome an obstacle and still fail, while the guy next to you waltzes right through it. After all the re-reading, practicing, and futile attempts to shift my apocalyptic outlook on my fate, comments like the one above made me believe that maybe I was meant to be this way.

When this happens, you have two options:

1.   Get angry and lose motivation.
2.   Realize that this person probably sucks at something you're really good at and you just have to work a little harder on this one.

Most people go with option one, which is why there is an abundance of ambitious kids, but an epidemic of underachieving adults. When people realize how hard greatness is, they settle for "eh, it's fine." Whether we realize it or not, the problem is we're constantly using the success of others to discredit our own potential—we're looking for every little thing that has ever helped someone calm their nerves, and we're getting down on ourselves when they don't work for us. We huff, puff, and stare disappointedly as fear reigns supreme in our lives.

For this reason, one of the most important things to drill into your brain and remember for the rest of your life is:

1. Failure will happen. A LOT.
2. Others will succeed at what you've failed at.
3. Your response to this failure will determine your success.

Failure becomes negative the second you make the decision to deem it "failure." If you elect instead to harness that failure, study it, figure out what went wrong, and discover how you can knock it out of the park next time, you turn it into opportunity. As my father says: "Never a failure, siempre (always) a lesson."

Which brings me to....

The Power of the Pivot

It could happen when you're standing on stage, trying to be conversational with the audience. It could happen when you've interviewed for a job you know you're perfect for, but you haven't heard back from the recruiter. It could happen at work, when your boss doesn't notice all the great work you've done, and skips on giving you a raise. You face an unfortunate situation, realize things didn't go your way, and accept it, saying, "That's life, I guess."

Sometimes, the best thing to do is to accept failure and move on. This applies in situations like trying to get back an ex-girlfriend and hearing: "I hate you. I never want to see you again. If you talk to me again, I'll file a restraining order against you." But in many other situations, we wave the white flag prematurely and give up a situation that could have very well ended positively. Sometimes, instead of giving up, you just have to *pivot*. Let me give you an example.

I have an African Grey Parrot named Greyson. He is super smart and a master imitator: able to impersonate me, my parents, singers he hears on the radio—his potential is limitless. When I was seventeen, my parents figured the bird needed to be on international primetime television, so the world could enjoy his many talents. Dad called the producers of the then most-watched Spanish nighttime entertainment show, "Sabado Gigante," to convince them to come to our house to get video footage of Greyson. A week later, the producers arrived with about eight members of their production crew.

Sabado Gigante film crew arrives
The Rosell home

The television crew set up enormous cameras, giant light fixtures, and a boom stand, all directed at Greyson. There were cables everywhere and the house was bursting with excitement. Once everything was set up, the decisive moment arrived.

What will Greyson say?

We stood there—tense, excited, eyes fixated on the little bird that would soon be an international icon. At first, Greyson frolicked around—proud, bathing in the light of impending stardom. He moved with swagger, shifting from branch to branch in his cage with the elegance of a dove. With each movement of his wings or click of his beak, his adoring audience's collective hearts raced in nervous anticipation. My parents and I couldn't stop smiling; we couldn't believe Greyson was about to be a star on the show everyone in our family watched every week!

But with each minute that passed, the crew's excitement dissipated. Two, five, seven minutes passed—Greyson did not seem interested in impressing the crew. After ten minutes, the crew started to get antsy. The boom operator's arms began to tremble violently and members of the camera crew started to sigh. I looked over at Dad and noticed he was drenched in sweat. He was looking straight at Greyson, quietly cheering him on. After fifteen minutes, the smiles were gone and everyone was checking their watches. After twenty minutes, the producers signaled for their team to pack up.

Dad paced nervously. One of the best public speakers I have ever seen, Dad is an expert at getting even the most intimidating audience on his side. He is loud, passionate, and has an uncanny ability to turn a potentially catastrophic performance situation into a success. One of his greatest skills is digging…that is, digging himself out of seemingly hopeless, humiliating situations, and turning them into something wonderful. As I watched him pace, deep in thought, I knew he would figure something out. Then, he gave me this look. There was a soccer ball in the corner of the room. I knew he was about to volunteer me to do something on camera.

At the time, I had a huge afro, had been wearing tight, punk rock clothes, with my leather biker jacket filled with studs and spikes I'd tacked on. My dad was about to volunteer me to be a circus clown for the cameras, until I sprinted towards him.

Me: Papa…Por favor…don't you dare.

Dad: Hijo, just juggle the soccer ball for dos minutos. They love it. They Latinos too, they love futbol. You look so crazy, like punker style. And if you juggle futbol, it'll be great. Make great TV. Man up, hijo.

Me: Papa, no…I can't. No….

Dad nodded disappointingly, whispered something about what a wimp I was under his breath, then announced to everyone in the room:

"Wait…We have a dog that sings!" he yelled. The crew members, who were sulking—likely because they were about to go home to their bosses with nothing, looked confused.

"Yes, this is something you cannot miss!"

The crew let out a sigh of relief. Two of them hugged each other and high-fived in celebration, shouting "Gracias a Dios!" (Thank the Lord!)

My father escorted them to the backyard where Tyson, our beloved boxer, sprinted towards them and excitedly greeted everyone with big licks. I tagged along, embarrassed, disappointed in myself. Fifteen minutes later, the lights were shining on Tyson, mics pointed towards him and about a dozen people stared intently.

Tyson's "singing" was more of a drawn-out howl in response to high-pitched sounds, but he only did it when I played guitar. As the crew waited, Dad stared at me, desperation in his eyes, signaling for me to hurry the hell up and get my guitar. I stared back, begging him not to make me do this. But I was doomed. I ran inside, and came out, my Yamaha acoustic in hand. I started playing "Twinkle, Twinkle, Little Star." Tyson stared at me, at the crew, then back at me. He opened his mouth, barked once, then hastily retreated to his doghouse and stayed there for the duration of their visit.

Well, that went well. Too bad, I guess! I surrendered.

Dad was saddened and humiliated, but he wasn't ready to give up. Before the camera crew started packing up again, he announced. "Wait! I make the ugliest faces in the world!"

They laughed dismissively and continued packing, but when they realized he was serious, they looked at each other, shrugged as if to say, "The flight doesn't leave for another eight hours, so why not," and started to set up again.

For a half hour, Dad sat in a chair, making a variety of grotesque facial expressions to the point where the veins on his neck started to pulsate. In front of all those lights, cameras, and boom stands, he had the entire group of "Sabado Gigante" crew members laughing their asses off. After the shoot, we all had drinks together, and had a glorious time.

"Sabado Gigante" never aired this segment, they never told us why. But we get the feeling all the employees have enjoyed this video countless times in the backrooms of the studio, perhaps as an icebreaker at new employee orientations. Dad's uncanny ability to pivot when things are going poorly resulted in something vastly more entertaining than they would have had—had Greyson talked or Tyson howled.

Moments after the crew left, we brought Tyson inside and I started playing guitar to him. He started howling, with a beautiful pitch that perfectly matched that of the song I was playing. In response to this, Greyson yelled "HAHA! I am the most intelligent bird in the world!"

Pivoting is a skill that didn't come naturally to me, but in order to progress as a human being, it's something I had to figure out how to do when things didn't go my way. When it came to public speaking, I didn't learn how to pivot until my commencement speech. And it wasn't so much a matter of defining a strategy for every circumstance, rather, it was developing a mindset that I should be ready to pivot when something goes wrong on stage. Things like a PowerPoint not working, forgetting your lines, or having a disinterested audience are all disadvantages that could be turned into advantages—with a simple pivot.

A part of overcoming fear comes down to what you do when you're standing in front of an audience. When you're up there, feeling exposed and contemplating how you're going to get through this speech, the mind does one of two things—either it gets extra-creative, creating ways to assure success and avoid disappointment, or it will say, "Screw this, I'm out!" and execute escape strategies. My tendency to try to soothe the effects of my fear was a prime example of the "Screw this, I'm out!" approach. Dad's was to get creative and figure out something that worked. He pivoted, when most people would have given up.

When it comes to public speaking, glossophobes tend to choose escape strategies instead of pivots. Here are some escape strategies we use to soothe our fears:

1. *Not making a connection with the audience*

Looking above the eye line of the audience, staring at a poster at the back of the room, or reading off a presentation document during your talk can all be nerve-reducing strategies—which create a barrier between you and your audience. This bad habit will make your fear harder to overcome in the long run.

If you don't connect with your audience, they'll become disinterested—even unfriendly. If you haven't engaged with them, made eye contact, and embraced the energetic exchange that can flow between speaker and audience, you won't notice when people are captivated by you, have questions, or are enjoying your presentation. This can add a layer of fear as you surmise that your audience isn't onside.

Instead of avoiding the audience, find faces that look friendly or interested, and keep your focus on them (but don't stare at them the whole time, that's creepy). Or, make it a fun challenge: find the faces in your audience that look completely disinterested, and make it your goal to capture their attention by the end of your speech!

2. *Fighting to hide your fear*

When you're scared out of your mind during a presentation, the last thing you want is for your audience to notice you're scared out of your mind. So, you do everything in your power to conceal that fact—you deepen your voice, use fancy words you wouldn't normally use, clutch the podium to disguise your trembling hands…all the while freaking out: *I hope they don't notice I'm terrified!*

The problem is that in addition to stressing out about the audience, the speech, your slides, and everything else, now you're increasing your anxiety and diluting your concentration as well. What you should be focused on: the audience's interest level. So, here's my advice: trying to hide your nervousness will likely only make things worse. Instead, focus on having fun: Insert a few tension-cutting jokes, fun tidbits, or questions for the audience. Good vibes are contagious.

3. Keeping it safe and painless

You're all set to rock your speech—your presentation deck is on point, you're comfortable with the material, and you've got a big bag of tricks you're going to try out to engage your audience. As you walk up to the podium, you start to notice little things that throw you off: there isn't a stand at the front of the room to put your papers on, people are looking at their phones, the audience isn't settling down. A seed of worry begins to sprout and you can't stop it from growing out of control. So, you scale back your expectations and reduce what you had planned to something safer and, hopefully, painless. To minimize the chances of bringing more stress to yourself, you limit your attempts to engage the audience, skip on jokes you had planned, and resort to reading off of text-heavy slides.

You take the easy route to avoid that extra stress, thus foregoing an amazing opportunity to test out new strategies and to take a big step towards overcoming your fear. In the end, you'll regret not trying harder to do well. Remember, the better your speech, the better you'll feel after it, and the better you'll feel before the next one.

4. *Rushing through a talk*

Rushing through your talk requires that you talk quickly. Talking quickly interferes with your breathing, which makes you sound agitated. Sounding agitated makes the audience look at you strangely. That ignites a nervous bomb in your stomach, which causes your anxiety to increase—tenfold. Your fear of public speaking intensifies and when that happens, your mind starts to race: anything could happen. Your skin might start to peel off. If you've lost a few layers of skin, you can't go outdoors, so you can't overcome your fear of public speaking.

Trust me on this one: don't rush. Avoid all of this, okay?

Before making any decision to give up, think about this: Do you want to look back at this moment and think: "I wonder where I'd be now if I'd tried a little harder?" or would you rather think, "I can't believe how amazing that was!" Do you think pivoting might be worth the extra effort?

But pivoting isn't always easy. Maybe you feel you're just not capable of doing any better, or you believe you don't deserve that opportunity that seems impossible to grasp. Well, in the following chapter, I'll share a story about two buddies of mine: One, an exceptional student in college struggled endlessly to find a job. The other, who barely had the grades required to graduate scored the job of his dreams. Guess which one learned how to pivot?

Risk This #14:
Poke a hole in your comfort bubble

Pick any of the options below, and accomplish it today:

1. Single and desperate for a date? Ask out the first girl/guy you think is cute.

2. It's end of semester and you're failing a class? Raise your hand in the middle of class and make a case for extra credit.

3. Been doing great work, and feel you deserve a raise? Craft a good pitch for why you should get a raise and present it to your boss.

If none of these apply, find something that rips you out of your comfort zone, something that you've been too scared to do—and just do it. If you succeed, that's fantastic! If you fail, even better. Figure out what you could have done better (ask around, replay your approach, etc.) and keep it in mind for next time.

CHAPTER 16:

Floyd and Clark –
Case Studies in Positivity

"Believe, hijo! Joo have to believe joo can achieve!"
— Mom

Due to Mom's stubborn quest to eliminate my negative attitude, any time I read or heard something on attitude or positivity, I'd cringe. If there's anything I've been lectured to the brim on, it is the "attitude is everything!" mantra. "Believe, hijo! Joo have to believe joo can achieve!" Mom preached, I squirmed.

When I was obsessing about reading all of those public speaking self-help books, I quickly grew tired of the "attitude talks." To me, success depended on skill and ability, not on an immeasurable factor like "attitude." I clung to the belief that those who work their entire lives to acquire fear-conquering skills claim the greatest opportunities, and that defeating fear was for natural-born fighters and achievers. I didn't have much experience and I sure as heck didn't consider myself an achiever, so logically, it would've been okay for me to settle for slightly less.

My subpar scores on midterm exams during college were partly to blame for my pessimistic views on positivity at that time. I'd try my best to be positive before exams—I'd smile, keep my head up, and repeat "I GOT THIS!" every time I started to question myself. When it was time to take the test, I'd sit down, pencil ready, big smile on my face. Within ten seconds of scanning the test, that smile would disappear, I'd be pissed off at the world, and my grade on that final would be the first letter of the four-letter word I blurted out upon learning I'd fallen short: "Crap!" (I had strict, grade-obsessed parents, no F's for me).

But everyone preaches about this positive thinking stuff—Thomas Jefferson stated that nothing can stop the man with the right mental attitude from achieving his goal. John C. Maxwell proclaimed that the greatest day in life is when we take total responsibility for our attitudes. Norman Vincent Peale taught that if we change our thoughts, we change our world. There are hundreds of thousands of quotes by the world's biggest achievers and greatest minds signifying the same thing: *Attitude has the power to change anything.*

But in the real world, "You've got to have the right attitude!" rarely carries more significance than overused phrases like "great work ethic," or "determined" on a job resume. But is "have a great attitude!" just a soft, fluffy catchphrase—or is it a key to overcoming fear?

I recently met with a close friend (let's call him Floyd) who, though well-qualified in his industry, is having a terrible time finding a job. In the span of our thirty-minute conversation, Floyd said:

I've been out of college for about six months now; apply to at least five jobs daily for a total of about 500 applications to date. I got four interviews and still haven't found a job. This sucks." .... "I have spent at least forty percent of my waking hours applying to positions online. My job has become applying for jobs, and I am the worst employee in the world." ... "Fifty applications this month, zero interviews. Just kill me now."

The thing is, Floyd is tremendously talented. He graduated with honors. He was active on campus, had a high GPA and great internships, and was a member of some prominent business clubs. Floyd knew how crucial building an attractive resume was in defining life after graduation, so he took the necessary measures to assure success.

But after graduating college, Floyd became a hermit chained to his computer. He spent most of his waking hours filling out applications, anxiously awaiting contact from recruiters. After about a month of no responses, he entered panic mode—he started feeling hopeless, convinced luck just wasn't on his side.

Another close friend of mine, Clark, didn't do so well in college—he half-assed homework assignments and negotiated his way to a 2.8 GPA by charming professors for grade bumps. While most students studied into the wee hours of the night, Clark stayed up watching "South Park" and "The Office" reruns, and made friends with the smartest kid in class to get tips on his homework assignments. His on-campus involvement consisted of consuming Beefy 5-Layer Burritos from Taco Bell' and taking twenty-minute bathroom breaks to scope out pretty girls around campus.

After nearly six years of mediocre educational performance at his university, Clark was ecstatic he'd finally acquired the piece of paper that certified him as smart enough to enter the workforce. Nevertheless, he didn't sit at home applying for jobs all day. He figured that to get something he'd never acquired (he'd tried and failed to get internships during college), he'd have to try something he'd never done. So instead of sitting all day submitting online applications, he decided to get creative.

As for Floyd, within six months of starting to apply to jobs and only four failed interviews to show for his efforts, he decided to postpone his dream of finding a job in marketing and instead, shifted his focus to applying to MBA programs. He was sick of school and never believed MBA programs were necessary. But after successive failures, he lost confidence in himself and in his ability to get a job he wanted (or any job for that matter). He was afraid that if more time passed, he'd end up working at McDonald's and living in his mom's basement.

Clark, on the other hand, was busy reaching out to recruiters, department heads, and attending industry events whenever he got the chance. He even started a marketing blog and referenced it in his cover letter and resume to show he truly had a passion for what he was applying for. He spent two months looking for jobs and soon afterwards, landed his dream job. He was underqualified when it came to the skills required, but he was able to convince the hiring manager with his creativity and passion. Against the odds, he achieved his goal by treating each failed application as a motivational kick in the butt to attempt different strategies.

Clark is the type of person people hate because he got the job so many better qualified people "deserved." But the thing is, Clark saw opportunity where Floyd saw hopelessness. Clark exuded self-assurance and drive; he was motivated, saw the path to where he wanted to be, and landed a job because he was willing to step out of his comfort zone. Consequently, people were attracted to his positivity.

This approach doesn't just apply to getting a job. It applies to getting dumped by your significant other, reacting to your co-worker getting the promotion you deserved, and—in our case—overcoming the fear of public speaking.

The idea that positivity leads to success is rooted in neuroscience. Neuroscience tells us that our pre-programmed subconscious minds dictate ninety-five percent of our thoughts. This means that, like Floyd and Clark, we don't treat each situation with a blank slate. Instead, we dig up past experiences, disappointments, and results and mix them all in with our current emotional state. We do this to decide what's worth fighting for and to predict an outcome. Floyd felt frustration and unworthiness each time he was rejected so naturally, he started to expect rejection.

It's been widely confirmed that there is a direct link between having a positive outlook and having feelings of inclusiveness, pain tolerance, and self-confidence. There is also a direct link between thinking positively and improving your creativity, problem-solving skills, and critical thinking abilities. When Clark was rejected, he reacted positively, was motivated to try harder, and so he attempted different strategies to attain the job he wanted.

In their widely-published journal article "Optimism, Coping, and Health: Assessment and Implications of Generalized Outcome Expectancies," Charles S. Carver and Michael F. Scheier studied situations where people encountered barriers. They discovered that each time a person faces a barrier, the brain starts to calculate probabilities of success. The conclusion of this process is the brain's outcome expectancy. It's the person's outcome expectancy that determines their behavior, thus determining the likelihood of each outcome.

For instance, during an argument with your significant other, emotion could consume you to such an extent that you might become focused on how you've been wronged and on proving your point. Any potential remedies might zoom right past your overly-occupied mind. Similarly, if you feel like a bucket of lard for eating a whole pizza by yourself and never exercising, and you feel plagued by feelings of hopelessness, then there is no room for you to create a solution to your problems.

Some people argue that they've concentrated all their mental energy on visualizing winning the lottery, getting their dream car, or finally getting their crush to like them, but they have seen no positive results. But here's the truth: positive thinking while sitting on the couch watching "Game of Thrones" will likely not result in success. Positive thinking is a required *supplement* to persistent effort, not something that will act on its own. In other words:

Positive thought → Belief your goal is attainable →
Necessary steps to achieve → Goal achieved

Notice the third step in the process to achieving your goal—it's the get-your-butt-to-work step. It's the action behind what was thought of in the first two steps. It's acting on the belief—no, the knowledge—that you can attain what you've been dreaming of. Clark nailed this process, while Floyd skipped steps one and two, and half-assed step three. Result? No achievement. For most of my fear-fighting life, I did the same thing as Floyd.

Next time you're questioning the importance of your mental approach, remember: Attitude is more important than facts, accomplishments, education, or the circumstances you find yourself in. Attitude is more critical than the way you look or the skills you have. The extraordinary thing about this is that it is entirely your decision what attitude you adopt at the start of any given day. Of course, there are things we can't control, but we have a constant decision to make regarding the attitude we embrace.

So, before you go on testing out different strategies for overcoming your fear, screw your head on straight. Prepare yourself mentally—not only for the worst but for the best, because the best is coming your way and you'd better be ready to take it.

Risk This #15: Adopt one good habit

Pick one habit you've wanted to adopt but for whatever myriad excuses, you haven't gotten around to yet. Keep it simple—don't promise you'll quit smoking or start running ten miles a day just yet. Whether it's waking up an hour earlier to plan your day, eliminating soda and chips from your diet, or giving three sincere compliments to people by nightfall every day, get started now. Stick to it. Once you hit a month, write down each of the three habits you adopted on a piece of paper with a description of how you feel now that you've made each of them a part of your daily routine.

CHAPTER 17:

Make Bertha Feel Stupid

"If failure is not an option, then neither is success."

— SETH GODIN

Bestselling author and entrepreneur Seth Godin is arguably one of the biggest influencers in marketing today. He isn't just a marketing genius in the traditional business sense, he's brilliant with the most important form of marketing too: marketing yourself. He's a highly sought-after public speaker, has best-selling books printed in over thirty-five languages, and demands a hefty fee for his speaking services.

I figured that being a world-renowned public speaker racking up $100,000+ per speech, he had to have something to say about overcoming the fear of public speaking. That's when I found Seth's blog post titled "Worst One Ever," which is about his first bout of speaking in front of an audience and how he was nervous, distracted, and not particularly well received. Even his closest friends and relatives in attendance had to admit that his presentation failed to engage—a performance not to be repeated. Fortunately for Godin (and his fans), he learned from this terrible performance.

The first time I read his post, I was about halfway through writing this book. I remembered everything I'd been through—the awful speeches, the unbearable nerves, the armpit-geysers. I decided I would include one of his quotes in my book and quickly extracted one from his blog post that fit in just right. But then I figured not everyone has heard of Seth Godin; so it would miss the mark with most of my readers. I kept thinking...*What if I called Seth Godin?*

I decided I would fight logic, sense, and my own Bertha's weak little voice to get our generation's greatest marketing mind and public speaker to talk to me on the phone. But just as with every other crazy idea I've had in my life, Bertha kicked in and tried to convince me that it would never happen. Our conversation went like this:

You want to interview Seth Godin? HA! He's too busy with his TED Talks and writing books of his own....

Nice to hear from you, Bertha. It's been a while....

Seth Godin is big time, Roy! Business Week called him the 'ultimate entrepreneur for the Information Age.' You know that. Don't even bother trying to contact him; you'll just make yourself look desperate!

I sat, deep in thought, Bertha and Paula waging war in my mind. Bertha did have a point...Seth probably doesn't have time to respond to all the wannabe writers trying to get a word with him. He didn't get to where he is sitting on his butt all day checking emails.... Bertha smiled—and grew an inch. After a few seconds of considering my options, I made my decision.

Dear Mr. Godin,

I know you're busy and must have a ridiculous amount of fan email to attend to, so I'll be brief. I fought the fear of public speaking for twelve years. It was so bad that I would cry myself to sleep nights before speeches, and I lived in a constant state of extreme stress and complete lack of confidence. It was messy.

Fast forward to the eleven years and nine-month mark of my battle. I got a call from the Dean's office at my university. I was informed that I was graduating top of my class. I was ecstatic. Then, I was notified that I would also be giving the commencement speech—to approximately 15,000 people. I went numb. Those next three months, I did everything I knew I should've been doing all along. I worked my ass off. After those three months, this was the prize:

https://www.youtube.com/watch?v=aS0_LiSaRIQ

So, to the point...if possible, I'd love to talk to you, even if just for five minutes over the phone. I want to ask you about your blog post about your first bout of public speaking in front of an audience.

Pardon the length of this email; I tried my best to be concise. I really hope to hear from you, Sir. Until then, have a wonderful time, Mr. Godin!

All my best,

Roy

The mouse pointer hovered over SEND, with my finger firmly pressed on the clicker. Then, I lifted my finger, which triggered a shriek of excitement and rampant arm flailing. I woke up at 7:00 a.m. the next morning and picked up my phone. New email from someone named Seth.

Hi Roy,

Could we talk about spiders instead? Happy to talk. I'm around this afternoon NY time.

I'll be damned! Not only did he respond to my email; he watched the video of my speech. Bertha scurried off, back to her dusty corner. I'd proved that I was capable and I'd once again silenced the voice that I'd always listened to so intently—that same voice that had almost made me bail out of my college graduation to avoid giving a speech. With each victory over Bertha, her voice became quieter and quieter. And, as I noted earlier, even when I didn't listen to her and failed anyway, those failures didn't fuel her, it only fueled my motivation to work harder.

I learned first-hand that doubtful thoughts get a lot louder the longer you go without silencing them. In the two years between my graduation speech and the time I wrote to Seth, I didn't do much that forced me outside of my comfort zone. As a result, the once-conquered Bertha started to emerge from her desolate corner again, in a desperate attempt to regain her once-dominant position in my life. Because of that, sending that email to Seth was harder than it would have been had I been more consistent with my fear-defying actions since graduation. But I knew that I could never allow her to regain her prominence, so I sent the email, which sent Bertha scuttling away.

In addition to the huge confidence boost and doubt-injuring benefits of pressing send on that email, I actually got the chance to speak with and learn from a public speaking giant. When I picked up the phone to dial, my heart was pounding in my throat. With each seemingly eternal pause between rings, I held my breath and sat completely still—conducting mini-prayers in my mind, hoping I wouldn't make a fool of myself.

I started the conversation with a little backstory about myself and why I was writing this book, the history of my glossophobia, details about my speech and….

"Roy. Let me cut you off. You've told me all this. How can I help you?"

My one chance to speak with one of the most sought-after speakers in the world, and I'd butchered the start of it. My heartbeat quickened. *Maybe this wasn't such a good idea.*

I could have panicked. Instead, I took a deep breath, and focused. I cut to the chase. I asked how he went from being a bad, nervous speaker (like I had been), to the public speaking genius he is (which I want to become). I told him my book was about my journey, to help others wake up and realize that they too can achieve their dreams.

Seth paused, then sighed. He explained that his first attempt at public speaking was a disaster because he didn't want to be there. He wasn't comfortable with the topic and, in the end, his negative approach to what he was talking about and the idea of talking altogether is what led ultimately to the lackluster performance.

It's the first time I felt I could relate to someone who was completely out of my league in every way imaginable (except for maybe hairstyles). It felt good that I had something in common with this public speaking master. Like him, the times I gave terrible speeches were the times I dreaded the thought of being on stage. But the presentations I performed well in were the ones I looked forward to, the ones in which I found something to like about the topic, and the ones I approached with a positive attitude, regardless of my nervousness.

"But let me express a danger with what you've told me about your book," Seth said.

Danger? I appreciate straightforwardness but damn it, Seth, don't kill my dreams!

I expected to hear a lot of the same things I'd heard when I told people I was writing a book about public speaking, including:

"Oh cool! Aren't there a ton of books about that already?"

"That's cute! Would a publisher pick up a book about public speaking, though?"

"Congrats! But why would someone read yours over one by a real public speaker?"

"Nice! Really think anyone would read it, though?"

Those comments had been annoying, and every time I'd heard one, I'd added that person's lack of belief in my project to the fire burning inside of me, driving me to succeed. If Seth had said something like that, I would've listened out of respect, then discarded it as soon as I hung up the phone.

But Seth knew better than to try to douse the drive of a passionate person. He asked, "How would someone go about learning to ride a bike?"

Hmm...Maybe get help from someone who knows how to ride a bike, use training wheels, take off training wheels, ride on a softer surface, move to a normal surface and voila, you're riding a bike.

"Yes. But people don't want to hear that. People email you because they want a shortcut. Give it to them straight—there isn't one."

This explained the phenomenon of people reaching out to me after seeing the YouTube video of my commencement speech, in an apparent state of desperation, only to ignore my carefully-crafted responses to their cries for help. People didn't like knowing they had to do the work. They didn't like hearing they had to improve their ability to approach situations with a positive outlook, banish their initial reaction to failure, and develop an action plan to achieve comfort on a stage. They wanted a pill, not a plan. They wanted results now, not in a couple of months.

I talked to Mr. Godin for six minutes. I didn't get a magical formula to overcoming the fear of public speaking. Looking back, I'm embarrassed to admit that a part of me expected one. I wasn't enlightened to a revolutionary new way to kill fear. But I was reminded of why people don't overcome their fears and why I didn't for so long either.

Looking back at my own battle, I was exactly the same as those people who were looking for a magic pill. I didn't want to hear that I needed to work for a few months to overcome my fear. I wanted an injection, a suppository, whatever, to make the transition from wimp to warrior as painless as possible. In addition, the last thing I wanted to hear was that getting over it all required putting myself in uncomfortable situations in which I could fail. I wanted a solution, and I didn't want to waste time working hard for it if it wasn't guaranteed. I needed it NOW. So, instead of just doing what I had to do, which was work a little harder to change myself so I could overcome my fear, I wasted years looking for an answer that I already had.

But, I figured it out eventually. It took twelve years to overcome my fear, because for most of that time, I was missing the mental aspect. I was allowing Bertha to influence every decision I made, I took my own hesitation as a sign that I should 'steer clear,' and I blamed everything and everyone whenever something went wrong for me. I hadn't made a promise to myself that I would keep fighting even when the going got tough, I didn't know how to bounce back stronger from disappointment and failure...I was just floating around aimlessly, with no focus or function, just hoping I'd stumble upon a cure for my phobias.

In those twelve years, I slowly but surely built the mental approach needed for success. Finally, three months before my college graduation, everything kicked into place. I was ready to rock. I created the Plan designed to control my fear.

Risk This #16: Eliminate a bad habit

Now that you've worked on adding a good habit to your everyday routine (Risk This #15), it's time to eliminate one bad one. Think of one habit you have—whether it's staying quiet during class or workplace discussions, drinking a couple of sodas per day, or not interacting enough with people around you. Pick one, start fixing it today, and set alarms for once a week for the next thirty days to check your progress.

Risk This #17: Hold yourself accountable

Now that you're ready for your fear-destroying formula, it's time to make giving up as painful as possible. Pick a date that you want to "enjoy" public speaking by, and make bets with five people that you will achieve this goal by then. You can bet money, favors, whatever will get you feeling like you simply cannot lose this bet.

PART 4

THE FEAR-DESTROYING FORMULA

CHAPTER 18:

Those Three Months

"Ay Dios Roy. Today, you complain that you don't have this, you don't have that so you can't do what joo want to do... Tomorrow, joo look back at today, and think: Ayyy Dios mio, I wish I still had this, and that, so I can achieve what I want to achieve."

— My Tia

As I've shared with you throughout this book, the journey towards those magical three months were challenging, sometimes grueling. Let's just say that I had to crawl through a lot of crap to get to the good stuff. But it wasn't always a slow, painful journey through crud—on some occasions, it was actually enjoyable. When I was twelve, for example, two years after the onset of my glossophobia, I decided that regardless of the dread I felt, I would have fun on stage during my next presentation. A week later, I got up from my seat in my seventh-grade history class, walked to the front of the classroom and conducted an entertaining speech. I was terrified before going up, but I had a wave of nostalgia—I felt excited on stage, the audience was responsive, attentive, and laughed at my jokes. That speech was a great success. But as you know, the fun didn't last. I became paralyzed by fear.

When I was fourteen and set to start high school in the Fall, I'd decided it was time to free myself from fear's grasp. *I can't be a scaredy-cat in high school! I won't make any friends!* So, I'd enrolled in speech class. All summer, I'd fantasized about all the opportunities that would open for me once I'd completed the class and become a confident public speaker. *I'm going to sign up for debate! I'll join model U.N.!* But that relentless positivity had turned to trepidation after my first failed presentation in high school: remember *Diffendoofer Day*? I'd dropped out of speech class. But that didn't save me from the dozen or so speeches I was forced to conduct throughout high school.

At seventeen, with a few months to go before high school graduation, I realized I had spent more time in the past four years crouched over a public toilet—unable to control my stomach due to the terror that prefaced every presentation—than I had working towards overcoming fear. Enough was enough. I recruited a couple of buddies and signed us up for a campus-wide karaoke competition. What ensued was probably the most nonsensical and cringe-worthy improvised performance in the history of karaoke. It was nerve-wracking—and we had a blast. Watch it here, if you're ready to cringe harder than you've ever cringed: www.youtube.com/watch?v=JKgeP_OOlvg.

But the triumph of our karaoke sensation didn't last. Like a landscaper who plants a beautiful garden, but stops watering it, I didn't build upon that onstage success, so the euphoria of victory drifted away and was, once again, replaced with doubt, discomfort, and dismay.

On the morning of my eighteenth birthday, just weeks before starting college, I finished memorizing a celebratory speech to give as a toast to my friends and family at my party. The speech was filled with humor and passion, certain to be memorable. Later that day, we were all seated in my back yard, when my cousin started chanting "Speech! Speech!" By his third obnoxious shout, everyone was chanting, "Speech, Roy! Speech!"

Grinning nervously at the head of the table, I rose reluctantly to my feet. I put my hand in my back pocket and thumbed the paper containing my script. I pulled the paper out of my pocket and faced my oppressors. But the paper stayed firmly grasped in my hand. Like so many other times in my life, Bertha barged in and, in the last second—I backed out to shouts of "What a lamo-o!" from my cousins and sympathetic pats on the back from my rosy-cheeked tia.

Once I started college, I knew I had to get it together. So, as I told you earlier, I joined an eardrum-shredding, government-bashing, society-rejecting, punk rock band as the lead guitarist. We started playing shows every weekend. I imagined this would be a fun opportunity to implement the lessons I was learning from the books. I'd be the band member who took charge, doing little chats and gabs between songs.

At the first show, before playing the first note, I stood in front of 250 or so punk rockers packed like sardines in a South-Central L.A. backyard. I grabbed the microphone, and looked out over a sea of spikey hair, leather jackets, and forty-ounce beer bottles. Everyone was eerily quiet, focused, hanging on my every breath, waiting for me to provide the fuel to kick-start the frenzy. I took a breath, opened my mouth, and, in the most un-punk rock way possible, turned to the lead singer and signaled: "You do it, please."

At the second show, I pounced on the microphone, looked out to the crowd dramatically, freaked, and let my guitar riff do the talking. In five years playing with the band, I never had the whatever-it-is to get up there and talk to the audience. Every time I was about to do it, I backed out.

From the ages of 18 to 22, I kept trying, but kept falling short. During my jobs and internships, I gave presentations here and there, but instead of striving for greatness, I just wanted to "get it over with" and avoid being vulnerable. Instead of impressing my audience, I suppressed my nervousness. Every time I'd do something I thought should work wonders but didn't, I'd reset my expectations. Eventually, I started expecting failure.

Throughout this battle, Bertha tempted me with an easy way out: *Accept reality, Roy—this is how you are meant to be.* I could float on, graduate college, pick a career where I didn't have to conduct presentations and—aside from a few obligatory instances—I'd never have to see the stage again.

But I didn't take that route.

Today, I love public speaking. I've achieved my goal and I know exactly what I was doing wrong all those years. I was missing something: doing a lot of the right things, but in the wrong way. I wasn't maximizing the fear-reducing potential. Worst of all, I was quitting just before the realizing real impact.

Those Three Months

If you've ever failed to stick to a diet or achieve a fitness goal, you've given into your-version-of-Bertha's tempting proposition to quit.

Day 1: You're obnoxiously excited, hyper-motivated, and have your meal and workout plan all set up. People may look at you and think, "Let's see how long this obsession lasts!"

Day 2: You're so sore you think you've damaged your body. You're hungry, but you know the struggle will be worth it. "No pain, no gain!" you scream at yourself in the bathroom mirror, as you're brushing your teeth.

Day 3: You haven't felt this good for as long as you can remember. You can't wait for the next workout. You bake a batch of cookies, then scoop them into the trash, laughing maniacally and yelling "Begone, demons!"

Day 4: You're fanatical about talking about your new diet, and forcing workout and diet recommendations on your disinterested family and friends. They nod and smile, saying things like "Oh, cool. I'll try that" to shut you up. But deep inside, they're egging you on.

Day 5: The cravings are strong, you start to feel like you require tacos to survive, but you conjure up the mental fortitude to stick to your plan.

Day 6: You start looking for motivation to keep you going and find just enough motivation to stay on track.

Day 7: You have a good, hard look at yourself in the mirror and realize you look the same, possibly worse, than you did on Day 1.

You'll probably push this diet and meal plan for another week, doing your best to convince yourself that it's just a matter of time before you start seeing results, but that's where Bertha will start to sound a lot more convincing. And if you listen to her arguments, you'll start to reason with yourself as to why it would be okay to quit:

Maybe this diet just isn't right for me...

I should do more research before I waste more time...

I'm just meant to be out of shape...

This is just the beginning; the hard part hasn't even started...

I really don't have the time to stick to this....

You might shake off these thoughts at first, but without determination and an unbreakable focus on the finish line, you'll be back to your old habits before you know it. Your plan, launched to great expectations, will fizzle out to the same ol' "would've," "could've," and "should've."

Bertha's voice and all her limiting propositions are rooted in fear. Though fear's purpose is to protect us from dangerous situations, like getting chased by a rabid pack of pit bulls, it often extends its ravenous reach into places it doesn't belong. Here, fear is an irrational invention of the mind, its sole purpose being to blur clarity, initiate negative thought patterns and, ultimately, force us to sacrifice our goals to protect us from—let's face it—non-existent threats.

Being afraid of public speaking is like fearing that imaginary pack of pit bulls. It's irrational.

This irrational fear stopped me from overcoming my fear for nearly twelve years. But in those enchanted three months, I implemented small changes to my approach. As a result, I succeeded.

The mental shift that occurred at the onset of my three-month battle was the turning point. To succeed, keep the following key points in mind:

1. Know you will succeed in achieving your goal

Even though you've screwed this up a thousand times, know that *this time*, at the end of all of your hard work, you will succeed. And even though you may have a creeping concern that your efforts will result in disappointment and that this will all just be a huge waste of time, know that every hiccup along the way might make you reconsider your approach, or give up altogether (much like the diet and workout scenario). But this time, you need to treat every misstep as a valuable lesson that will help you reach your goal quicker.

2. Dream less, sacrifice more

My whole life, I wished, hoped, and prayed I would get over my fear. I pictured myself presenting to thousands of people, speaking confidently, facing an audience that loved every minute of my presentation. You've probably spent a lot of time hoping and dreaming for a 'better you' as well. Now is the time to realize that you could dream all you want, be relentlessly positive, and have an undying belief that you will achieve your dreams. But without risk and sacrifice, you won't make any progress. To attain your goal, you must turn dreaming into doing, with consistent, persistent, unremitting ACTION.

3. Dump analysis paralysis

The toast I avoided at my eighteenth birthday, the riot-inducing quips I never made to punk rock audiences, the executives I never spoke to at networking events—these are prime examples of *analysis paralysis*. Society teaches us to be cautious: to think before we speak or act, to consider all potential outcomes, and to understand the how-to minutiae of doing something before actually doing it. What many of us fail to realize is that this only applies to major life choices and potentially life-threatening situations—such as crossing the street or deciding whether to eat that yummy-looking forest mushroom on your camping trip. To overcome your fear, you're going to have to eliminate the tendency to analyze before acting. Instead, implement the "count to three" strategy. Once you do this, you'll eliminate those last minute, fear-driven decisions to tame your speeches or avoid risky decisions to stay "safe." (Do not, however, eat that mushroom.)

4. Cease the blame game

Remember the blame game? Well, it's time to stop blaming a busy schedule, genetics, illness, lack of opportunities, a weird haircut, or any person, place, or thing for your problems. Make YOU 100 percent responsible for YOUR progress. Never again use "I don't have any opportunities to present" or "I can't find even an extra minute for anything!" as excuses for your lack of progress. If you can't find that opportunity, it means you're not working hard enough to make it happen.

5. Change your reaction to fear

Fear gets overwhelming when you're about to do things that will vanquish it. So, the way to weaken fear is to continuously do things that awaken it. When you feel fear intensifying, that because it's trying to wrap its creepy little claws around your neck and choke the positivity out of you. To take away fear's power, go full steam ahead. Whether you fantasize about blowing the minds of your audience by the end of your talk or causing half the room to roll around laughing, set your goals and do everything possible to achieve them. When you fail, figure out what you could have done better, then keep trying.

6. Stop caring about the public's reactions

I hated the idea of people thinking I was stupid because of some screw up I committed on stage. So, I steered clear of taking risks. Instead of aiming for *phenomenal*, I aimed for *safe*. As I result, I nearly bored my audience into a collective coma every time I presented. If you want to avoid this, you need to stop obsessing about what the audience thinks about you, why they're looking at their phones instead of listening to you, or why they are so damned intimidating. By obsessing over these things, you lose focus on creating the one thing that'll make any audience love you: a great speech. Once you focus your attention on your speech, they'll enjoy your presentation more.

7. Eliminate conditional language from your thought process

- I'll give it a shot...
- I think I can do it...

- I'm not sure...

- It should work...

- What if…

- If only...

- I don't know if I can...

- I'll try my best...

- I'll do it, but...

- I wish I could do it!

- If I'd just....

Every condition you set on yourself will hold you back from progressing. To move forward, you must eliminate these words from your vocabulary.

Once you prep your mind to abide by these seven rules, you'll be ready to create your action plan and conquer your fear. If you want to drastically increase your chances of staying focused and minimize the chances of quitting, you need a plan. "Winging it" will only get you so far.

When going through the formula I present in the following chapters, you need cojones. Having cojones means considering the potential dangers, debilitating fears, and discomfort—and then going through with it anyway. Having cojones means seeing the ultimate goal, seeing the barriers between you and that goal, and saying, "Screw it—I'm all in."

So, for me, in those three months, anytime I felt like taking a step back, slowing down, or trying something easier while implementing the formula, I had to stay hyper-focused and motivated to keep going. Because of my decision to push forth in difficult moments, I was able to rid myself of glossophobia.

Regardless of how busy you might be, don't use it as an escuse to estop. An inability to manage your time and making excuses are two terrible habits. Don't combine them by saying you don't have the time. Come hell or high water, once you decide it's time to defeat your fear, you must keep going. Nervousness has been your signal to bail. From this moment on, nervousness is your calling. You're going to need the fervent determination of a one-legged man in an ass-kicking contest to win this battle.

Without further ado….vamos!

Risk This #18: Uncover your stubbornness

Keeping in mind that many of us have the tendency to get defensive when it comes to pointing out weaknesses in ourselves, go through the list of seven items again and write down the following:

One example of how you committed each item. For instance, for number 3, give an example of a time you didn't take action because of over-analyzing a situation.

Write one sentence for each item on the list of how you are going to do improve. For instance, for number 7, list how you are going to catch yourself using conditional language and how you'll stop it from happening again.

CHAPTER 19:

Creating the Action Plan

"When managed, fear is a gift. Yes, it's a gift that comes with an awful instruction manual and it requires diligence, creativity, and persistence to build it to your liking. But once you dedicate yourself to putting in the work, it will be one of the greatest gifts you'll receive."

— ME, after finally figuring out how to use fear to my advantage

Y ou may be thinking: "About damn time, Roy! I've had enough of your weird anecdotes and obscene metaphors. I've made The Pact, I'm aware that I'll probably experience failure along the way and may feel levels of fear I've never felt before—I'm totally cool with all of that. I'm ready for action!"

With this new mentality, you're more than two-thirds through your battle. The excuses for why you haven't controlled your fear, justifications for why you're not fit to give good speeches, and the progress-killing tactics you employ to avoid doing things that would help you advance are now a thing of the past. Now that your mind is finally in line with your goals, it's time for the final step: creating and acting on the action plan to tame your fear.

There are five quick steps needed to personalize your plan. First, you'll need to write down all the situations that make you uncomfortable. Second, you'll rate each of the fear-causing situations you listed on a 1-10 Fear Scale. Third, you'll take a deep look at your list and consolidate it so that each item will be a major contributor to your progress. Fourth, you'll group items so that your list is actionable. Finally, you'll put the groups you created in order so each step is a progression.

Step 1: Write down situations that make you uncomfortable.

Dig deeply into your mind and pull out all the situations that make your heart thump with nervous anticipation and let them bleed out onto a piece of paper. Do your best to write down as many situations that make you uncomfortable as you can, even if they're not directly related to public speaking. More importantly, include social, romantic, professional, or any other scenarios that hold you back from becoming the well-rounded person you want to be. Whether it causes a moderate level of discomfort or its mere mention makes you feel like you've been punched in the throat, list everything that comes to mind.

When listing your situations, be descriptive—a work talk to a room of five associates will cause a different level of stress than a large-scale presentation to fifty, so separate those items instead of combining them under a single category. In addition, realize that if you have set a date by which you want to complete your action plan, don't include any situations that will take longer than your target time to accomplish.

Having everything that makes you uncomfortable laid out in one place will help you organize your action plan to overcome your fear.

To help you kick start your list, I've included sixteen items from my own list of twenty-five. I created this list on the first day of those three months and these items led to me taming my fear of public speaking. If you have more than twenty-five items, wonderful! The more you have to work with, the better.

- Asking a question in class
- Giving a wrong answer in class
- Volunteering to present a current event topic in class
- Speaking up in a staff meeting at work
- Conducting a prepared presentation at a work meeting
- Starting a conversation with an executive at a networking event
- Starting conversations with strangers (on the street, in elevators, at the supermarket, etc.)
- Presenting a prepared speech to a small group (< thirty)
- Presenting a prepared speech to a large group (> thirty)
- Presenting a spontaneous speech/talk to a small group
- Presenting a spontaneous speech/talk to a large group
- Cold calling people over the phone
- Calling people you haven't talked to in years
- Giving team talks during your soccer games
- Singing and playing guitar in front of people
- Singing poorly in front of people.

Once you've laid out your list, go through it to make sure you have included the obvious items (giving a speech to thirty +, presenting a current event topic) and also throw in some curveballs. My curveballs include giving a wrong answer in class and singing poorly in front of people. Once you've done this, you'll have the list containing everything that has been holding you back from being the person you want to be.

Step 2: Rate each fear and put in order.

Now it's time to rank these items by "Fear-Rating." To accurately rate each item, refer to the following fear scale. The scale uses public speaking as the activity, but you can plug in any of the items on your list:

FEAR SCALE (Public Speaking)

1-3 – Low Level of Healthy Fear: The idea of giving a presentation makes your heart race, but the feeling upon learning of an impending speech is anticipation. Having this range of fear is the least stressful, but it is slightly lower than the optimal level to ignite top performances.

4-6 – Moderate Level of Healthy Fear: Like a thrill-seeker waiting in line to bungee jump, presentations make you nervous, but in the best way possible. Based on my experience giving speeches, the lower end of this range is the prime level of fear for giving speeches.

7-8 – High Level of Unhealthy Fear: This is the type of anxiety associated with waiting for the results of an STD test after a regret-producing weekend in Vegas. You accept that public speaking is a fixture for success, but the stress that presentations cause has a negative impact on your preparation and other factors in your life.

9 – Dread: You look for any excuse to avoid public speaking even if it means failing in class or missing out on opportunities. For speaking assignments you can't miss, getting back to your seat as quickly as possible is your main goal.

10 – Scared Speechless: Line up a polished podium and a kiddie pool filled with brown recluse spiders side by side and you'll be in that pool in a second. This level of fear not only causes health problems, it also negatively affects your relationships and sets you up to squander opportunities.

For each item on your list, the aim is to get out of the 7-10 range and keep your fear in the 3-5 range. Anything less than a 3 and you miss out on the countless benefits of a healthy level of fear. Anything higher than a 6 and you're putting yourself through unnecessary stress to accomplish tasks. The fear should work for you and motivate you, not diminish you.

Fear, when controlled, is a wonderful, motivating, thrilling thing. When managed, fear is a gift. Yes, it's a gift that comes with an awful instruction manual and requires diligence, creativity, and persistence to shape it to your liking. But once you dedicate yourself to putting in the work, it will be one of the greatest gifts you'll ever receive.

Finalizing Your Action Plan

Now that you've assigned a fear rating to all the situations that have haunted you in your journey to overcoming your fear, it's time to make that list actionable. Steps 3 through 5 will do exactly that, then I'll provide additional recommendations to maximize the effectiveness of the action plan.

Step 3: Make your list stronger by eliminating the excess.

Start with eliminating anything with a fear rating of 4 or less. Remember, you shouldn't strive to eliminate fear completely—by doing that, you'd be eliminating the extra boost of motivation you need in order to excel. Secondly, remove anything you won't realistically be able to do within the next three months. For instance, in my original list I had "giving sales pitches to investors" as an 8-rated fear. Since my goal was to learn to control my fear within three months and this would have taken much longer to realize, I had to cross off that item for the time being.

Step 4: Grouping to make your list actionable.

Assuming you didn't fill your list with items at a 4 or below rating, you should have ten + situations that make you uncomfortable (if you don't, add items until you have a minimum of ten).

Combine items that cause similar levels of anxiety and that can be done within a couple of days of each other. For instance; asking a question in class, giving a wrong answer in class, and volunteering to present a current event topic in class all conjure similar levels of fear and can be done within days of each other, so group them together. Same goes for speaking up in staff meetings, conducting a prepared presentation at a work meeting, and starting a conversation with an executive at a networking event. Not every item will have a group and not every group will have the same number of items in it.

Step 5: Put all your items in an order to create progression.

Once you've grouped together what you can, order your list starting with the items you fear least, ending with your ultimate goal. Strive to create increasing levels of fear within each group, as well as for the list as a whole. I've included my own list below for reference:

1. Starting conversations with strangers in various locations (5.5 fear rating).

2. Asking questions in class (5.5), answering questions in class (6), giving a wrong answer in class (7).

3. Speaking up in staff meetings (6.5), starting a conversation with an executive at a networking event (6.5), volunteering to conduct a prepared presentation at work (7.5).

4. Cold calling strangers (6.5), calling people I haven't talked to in several years (7), volunteering to present a current event topic (7.5).

5. Singing and playing guitar in front of people (8), singing poorly in front of people (9).

6. Presenting a prepared speech to a small group (< thirty people) (8.5).

7. Presenting a prepared speech to a large group (> thirty) (9).

8. Presenting a spontaneous speech/improv talk to a small group (9).

9. Presenting a spontaneous speech/improv talk to a large group (9.5).

As you can see, all the similar items have been grouped and ordered from least to most fear-inducing.

Improving Other Aspects of Your Life Through Your List

When I made my original list, I knew that if I was going to spend a few months working on it, I should use it to improve aspects of my life I wasn't satisfied with. I felt I had fallen into a routine, that I wasn't doing anything spontaneous or crazy anymore. As a result, I added a couple of tasks around doing something outrageous. When I was younger, I had some pretty gnarly dance moves—so gnarly in fact, I once executed them on stage in front of an audience. I got raucous applause and people chanted my name. I decided to revive my dance moves, so I added "start and be the center of a dance circle (8)" to my list.

Another aspect of my life I wasn't satisfied with was my lack of professional network connections. To solve this, I added "introduce myself and hold conversations with executives at work (6.5)." As a direct result, I ended up making friends in high places whom I am still in contact with today.

Don't be afraid to sprinkle things in as you think of them. Making a toast, doing interviews, going to a party/club/bar and talking to X number of people, singing aloud while walking down the street, playing guitar, and singing in an open area.... Add it, rate it, group it—and do it!

Risk This #19: Bet on your future

Make a bet with someone close to you pertaining to your fear-controlling formula. Set a final goal, a date (set a reminder for it on your phone) and bet that you'll achieve it by that day or you owe your buddy a fancy dinner!

CHAPTER 20:

The Attack

Mom: *Que vas a hacer hoy, hijo? (What are you going to do today, son?)*

Me: *I'm just waging war on my fear, Mom. I made an action plan and I'm finally going to defeat my glossophobia. It's going to get messy.*

Mom: *Okay, hijo, que bueno (that's good). Wear sunblock, okay?*

Me: *What does sunblock have to do with this? Did you even hear what I said?*

Mom: *Si, hijo. Now that joo gonna beat fear, joo have to keep your skeen healthy. So, when you do espeeches to thousands of people, all the chicas will say "ooohhh Roy has beautiful skeen!"*

Ask yourself how many times in your life you've started to work towards a goal, only to let your motivation fade to oblivion. For me, it happened with an entrepreneurial venture I'd worked on tirelessly and made tremendous progress with. Then, I hit a standstill when I ran into a difficult situation. It happened countless other times with learning new skills, getting in shape, sticking with diets, completing career-related certification programs, and much more.

One of the main reasons I deserted my goals in these instances was that I didn't know what to do when I hit a wall. With public speaking, it has always been not having the opportunity to speak as frequently as I needed to, to control my fear. I set out a plan for myself, but I didn't put much thought into how I would accomplish each part of the plan.

Knowing when, where, and how you will accomplish each item on your list are important factors in achieving success. For items that require giving a speech to an audience, for example, will you conduct your speech through Toastmasters¨? At work meetings? At City Council events? If you have impromptu speeches on your list: Will you make your speech in a classroom setting? Create a makeshift podium on the street? Try it out at an upcoming work dinner? Before you put your list into action, go down your list point by point and finalize the logistics for as many items as you can. The purpose of doing this is to minimize the time you spend "figuring out the details" of how you're going to progress after you've already begun to take action.

For my list, I did the following:

1. Starting conversations with strangers (5.5 fear rating).

How: Take every opportunity at school, at work, at the supermarket, on vacation, on the streets—everywhere—to start up a conversation.

2. Asking questions in class (5.5), answering questions in class (6), giving a wrong answer in class (7).

How: Ask and answer (sometimes incorrectly on-purpose) at least once in every class session I'm in. On weekends, find at least one Meet Up (www. meetup.com) or local library event to attend and to ask/answer questions in.

3. Speaking up in staff meetings (6.5), starting a conversation with an executive at a networking event (6.5), volunteering to conduct a prepared presentation at work (7.5).

How: Study meeting topics and ask questions, answer questions, and present at every work meeting I attend (discuss with boss and get approval). Start conversations with every executive in the office, especially those I never speak to. Start conversations with executives from other building tenants. Find and RSVP to professional networking events via *meetup. com*, *eventbrite.com*, and other event listing sites, and volunteer to do short presentations on the topics discussed. Find and RSVP to career fairs.

4. Cold calling strangers (6.5), calling people I haven't talked to in several years (7), volunteering to present a current event topic (7.5).

How: For cold calling, pick random names from phonebook or online number directory and call them. Tell them exactly why I'm calling and talk for a few minutes if possible. Talk to at least fifteen strangers. For people I haven't talked to in years, go through my address book and randomly pick fifteen names to call and talk about a nice memory I had with that person.

For current event topic, go through same avenues (work; school; online meetup directories; Toastmasters; city events; and library events) and offer to do a short, current event presentation for each one.

5. *Singing and playing guitar in front of people (8), singing poorly in front of people (9).*

How: Learn a song and play it for my family at home. Take guitar to school and play in main quad. Take guitar to old town Pasadena or Downtown Los Angeles and play in the street. Start off trying really hard to sing/play well, then spend some time singing out of tune.

6. *Presenting a prepared speech to a small group (less than 30 people) (8.5).*

How: Throw a small BBQ at home, then give a prepared toast. Give a toast at extended family dinner/gatherings. Contact all local Toastmasters clubs, public speaking meetups, and email all professors for classes I'm taking, explaining my mission and asking for a chance to speak. Contact clubs on campus and ask to speak about a related subject. Call for meetings at work to present findings/ideas/etc. Contact local libraries for opportunities to present.

7. *Presenting a prepared speech to a large group (thirty+) (9).*

How: Same as #6. Add city council events to the mix (contact city for "open mic" schedule).

8. Presenting a spontaneous speech/improv talk to a small group (9).

How: Same as #7.

9. Presenting a spontaneous speech/improv talk to a large group (9.5).

How: Same as #7.

There are so many ways to give a presentation and no matter what is on your list, you should never run out of ideas of how you're going to accomplish the task in a timely manner. It takes an extra half hour to research and discover opportunities to speak, even if they're not formal presentations to a seated audience. Stay completely committed to your decision to fight your fear and stay flexible in your approach. Just because a planned speech falls through doesn't mean you have to wait weeks until you have another one lined up.

No part of this list is meant to confine you. The purpose of this list is to provide you with a ladder you can climb to face your fear. As you get started, keep these important rules in mind:

1. Set realistic expectations.

As previously mentioned, you shouldn't strive to eliminate your fear, you should only strive to reduce it to a healthy level. Things like spontaneous presentations to a large group will always be nerve-wracking, but there's a difference between wanting to jump off a cliff and feeling intense butterflies in your stomach before a presentation. Aim to achieve the latter.

2. Don't move on from a task until you've become comfortable doing it.

The first task on my list was to start conversations with strangers—my first couple of attempts were pretty disastrous. I was overthinking everything and as a result my approach felt unnatural and the conversations that ensued were painfully awkward. This, in turn, made me want to avoid the situation even more. At that point, I could have easily said to myself: *Roy. You've already tried this three times and you still feel like a crippled gazelle surrounded by blood-thirsty hyenas. We've wasted enough time on this one, let's move on!*

No, no, Roy. Joo cut that nonsense, right now. Instead of moving on when I wasn't seeing the progress I expected, I did some research on how I could do it better and I kept at it. And, after a couple more attempts, my fear level started to wane and maintaining conversations became more natural. So, to maximize your chances of being successful with your list, stay with the step you are on until your fear has reduced to a level you're comfortable with.

3. Skip extended breaks.

One way to make the process of overcoming your fear as long and painful as possible is to take extended breaks. It's easy to take a few days off when you just feel like relaxing at home after a long week at work. It's also easy to put your action list on pause for a week when you go on a family vacation. There are always going to be distractions to derail your progress and justifications to put everything on hold. Instead of taking it easy, understand that you'll just need to work a little harder these next months to achieve your goal. It'll be far more rewarding in the long run to skip the extended breaks and constantly seek opportunities to get yourself out of your comfort zone.

4. Concentrate on quality, not completion.

Sometimes, the desire to feel the satisfaction associated with crossing items off your list could lead to taking shortcuts to complete items with minimal effort. Don't give in to this temptation. Instead of looking for the quickest ways to cross items off your list, look for ways to perform each one as often as possible and to improve each time you perform it. If one of your items is starting conversations with strangers, don't do one of these and think it's enough to cross it off your list:

You: "Hi, how are you?"

Poor soul: "Good and you?"

You: "I'm good too..." (both awkwardly look down at phones).

Instead, find ways to make that conversation interesting and mutually beneficial. This also goes for giving speeches. Do everything in your power to make each speech as intriguing, entertaining, and memorable as you can for audience—and for yourself.

5. Make habits.

Don't lose momentum by just running through this list once and being done with it. Many items are things you should be doing regularly. For almost every item on my list, I feared them because I avoided them. The more I avoided them, the more they became terrifying tasks. So, once you've crossed off an item, figure out a way to integrate it into your daily life. For instance, for talking to strangers, just make it a habit to say "Hi" to people in elevators, ask how their day is going, compliment their hairstyle or clothing. It's a tiny change that will make a big difference in your progress (and hopefully other people's days).

6. Track your progress.

Some people (myself included) are more likely to accomplish tasks if they have a daily checklist to hold them accountable. Keep a daily log similar to the one I've included below (sample answers provided).

Date: 08/31 (Day 3)

Tasks for today:

   Task 1: Ask questions in class.

   Task 2: Answer questions in class.

   Task 3: Give wrong answer in class.

How many times you did Task 1: 3

How you felt before task (include fear ranking):

   I was hesitant to ask my first question, kept looking for the perfect opportunity. Fear was about a 5.5. Finally decided to just do it.

How you felt after task (include fear ranking):

   About a 3. Relieved, excited, hungry to ask more questions. Realized how good it feels to become an active participant in class conversations.

How many times you did Task 2: 2

How you felt before:

Nervous, about a 6. I wasn't entirely confident with the topic being discussed, but decided to shoot my hand in the air the first opportunity I got.

How you felt after:

Relieved (about a 3.5). For both of my responses, I gave an answer that at least resembled something correct. It felt great getting props from the professor as I'm usually pretty uninvolved during class discussions.

How many times you did Task 3: 1

How you felt before:

About a 7. After answering correctly twice, I was feeling good about the impression I've made. I was tempted to replace this task with more of Task 2. But I decided to raise my hand no matter what the next question was and give a wrong answer.

How you felt after:

Uncomfortable and awkward. A little better than before, but still at about a 5.5 fear rating. The question was something I knew the answer to, so it felt strange giving a wrong one.

How many times you did Task 4: 2

Tasks I'm comfortable with now: 1 and 2

Tasks that need to be redone: Task 3

If at the end of the day you answered "zero" to any of the "how many times you did Task __?" questions, get up out of bed and do it. If that task is not doable, replace it with another task for today and double up on your original task for the next day. In future, don't skip on your objectives unless absolutely necessary.

With this list, you'll know you're in danger of failing when you find yourself postponing tasks, replacing one task with another, or being "too busy" to complete a task. When you're scared, nervous, or questioning whether you're capable of doing a task, know that this is your 'Bertha' trying to derail you. Don't allow your doubts to kill your goals. If you don't feel renewed after doing a task for three or four days, don't stress. This is shock treatment; do it until it's no longer a shock. For some (myself included), it might take longer than you want—keep at it!

As noted earlier, even after I suffered for most of my life, those last three months felt like a walk in the park. I mean a walk in a park in South Central Los Angeles during a scheduled gang war. This was never meant to be easy.

But there are little things out there that will make the struggle a bit more tolerable. One thing that you may find difficult is finding consistent opportunities to speak in front of an audience. Happily, there is a well-known organization to achieve this—and it's the topic of the upcoming chapter. Cheers!

CHAPTER 21

Toastmasters™: What to Know

*"The only thing standing between you and your goal is the bullshit story
you keep telling yourself as to why you can't achieve it."*

—JORDAN BELFORT, motivational speaker and stockbroker

W hen working on your list, you are frequently going to need opportunities to present speeches. As noted, I attended open sessions at City Council meetings, I volunteered at school and work, I even made speechifying part of my entrepreneurial venture. Maybe you don't have the resources (such as being at school or having the time to start up your own company) to consistently conduct presentations—so for you, there's Toastmasters".

Toastmasters is a non-profit organization that operates clubs worldwide for the purpose of helping people improve their public speaking skills. Whether you're in Dublin, New York, or Budapest, chances are you're just a few miles away from the meeting place of your local Toastmasters" club. I actually have about eight different Toastmasters" clubs to choose from within a fifteen-mile radius of my house!

If you're suffering from any sort of speech-related anxiety, you've probably had your eardrums pounded with screams of "Toastmasters! Join Toastmasters! It'll change your life! OMG Toastmasters!" From college professors to your boss to your know-it-all neighbor, everyone seems to swear by these proclaimed masters of toasts for curing oratory woes. But is it really as great as people say it is?

Throughout the years, I've come across hundreds of people who have been involved with the organization. There are the die-hard ambassadors who claim they'd be social hermits residing in a sewer had it not been for Toastmasters˝, and others who say it freed them from glossophobia's death grip.

They're not wrong—Toastmasters˝ is pretty amazing. It gives us exactly what we need to overcome our fear: a platform to face our fears on a consistent basis and to exercise our public speaking muscles. Almost as importantly, it gives us access to a group of people that are eager to nudge us along on our journeys. Fellow Toasters will give you valuable feedback on your presentations, motivate you to keep pushing forward, and help lay out the path for you to become an effective speaker.

So, if this club is so great, why is public speaking still a source of terror for so many people? There are Toastmasters˝ locations in every corner of the earth, so accessibility to its meetings isn't an issue. To top it off, it's affordable.

I've tried Toastmasters˝. I've attended meetings at four different clubs, and though I didn't stick around with any of them for more than a couple of months, I was able to get a good understanding of what it is about organization that people love—and that others dislike. From the information I've gathered, there are three things that someone who has a fear of public speaking needs to be prepared for when attending a meeting:

The Expertise Level

There I was, a terrified seventeen-year-old kid, hoping there would be a couple of people I could relate to at the Toastmasters™ meeting. Instead, I watched presenter after presenter walk up to the podium, heads held high, and conduct the type of speeches you'd see a presidential candidate give during an election campaign. There was no way in hell these guys had glossophobia, I thought. Aside from a couple of people that were super self-conscious about their mastery of the English language, it seemed like I was the only one struggling with public speaking.

Even though it was about a decade ago, I vividly recall the first speech I watched at my first meeting. It was a tall, chubby guy with shifty eyes and a big smile. He was part of some acai juice MLM (multi-level marketing) pyramid scheme and he asked if he could present the sales pitch that he gives to potential "business partners" to convince them to sign up to sell glass bottles of this "miraculous" super juice.

At the time, I was already well aware of the existence of these pyramid schemes and could predict a pitch coming a mile away. After all, I was raised to be distrusting of things that sounded "too good to be true," so I was less prone than most to fall in to these traps.

When the club meeting ended that night and Dad arrived at the scene to pick me up, I got in the car, slammed the door shut and yelled, "Papa!

How would you like to retire by forty!?" My dad responded, "Hijo, estas loco (are you crazy)? I'm sixty-three years old."

"Papa, that's fine, but how would you like to change your health forever?!"

The guy gave such a kick-ass speech that common sense went straight out the window and I was sold on his offering. The next meeting, I brought Dad along. He ended up signing up with this guy, a decision we regret to this day.

After two meetings with my first club, I quit. The reason: I wasn't mentally prepared for the speaking level of the other club members. I had jumped straight into trying to kill my fear from the get go, without first preparing myself mentally to handle discomfort and unexpected realities. Doubt overcame me, and I concluded that Toastmasters was too high-level for me. I had to start small.

The Formality

Awkward standing ovations, excessively positive feedback, and explosive laughter follow the worst of jokes at Toastmasters. Four years after my first visit to a chapter meeting, I gave Toastmasters a second shot, this time with a different chapter. It was a great club: organized, a good mix of people, and a lot of opportunities to network. One of the presenters, a tan Caucasian male in his sixties sporting a funky Hawaiian shirt, walked up to the podium and kicked off his speech with something along the lines of "Ho ho! What a good-looking crowd, it sure is getting hot in here!" He stuck his fingers in his collar, pulled outward and made a strange "eeeeeeeeek!" sound. I cringed, but everyone responded with boisterous laughter. Based on the explosiveness of the laughter, I assumed it was an "in" joke and that as a new member I was bound to run in to these.

Less than a minute later, he made another joke, this time saying something about people thinking he is Hawaiian because he likes wearing Hawaiian shirts, then followed it with, "I'm not a Hawaiian, I'm as American as it gets, Dudes and Dudettes!" Everyone roared—people were wiping their eyes they were laughing so hard. I cringed so hard, I'm pretty sure my face started to swell. The fact that he didn't realize Hawaii is in the United States made me a little nervous.

When he finished his painfully awkward presentation, everyone rose to their feet and applauded for about thirty seconds straight. *A standing ovation?* I thought. *Why?!* Well…Welcome to Toastmasters! This is, at least in my experience, expected audience behavior. This is good and bad: good because it eliminates the possibility that there will be mean people in the crowd whispering to their friends and having giggle parades while you speak; bad because there's a possibility that if you get accustomed to this ideal audience, you'll panic when you have to deal with a disinterested, disrespectful crowd.

The Concentration

As I said earlier, before my first Toastmasters meeting, I thought I was going to a place full of glossophobes like me and that a bulk of each meeting would be spent on figuring out techniques to overcome our shared fear... not necessarily. Not only did most club goers appear comfortable with public speaking, it didn't seem like the curriculum was designed to target fear. Because glossophobes are prone to creating excuses for not having to face their fears, the fact that the class's concentration is on presentation technique rather than on the fear itself could provide fuel for your excuse-making fire.

I thought that in order to eliminate my fear, I had to be in a rigorous, hyper-targeted program specifically designed to kill fear as quickly and assuredly as possible. But here I was, listening to the master of ceremonies discuss the importance of a good introduction.

Unfortunately, this detail led to me quitting Toastmasters that second time I tried it out. It took another two years before I set foot in another meeting.

Despite these quirks, I highly recommend joining. Why? Because the excuses above were ones I made when I wasn't mentally prepared to deal with the difficulties associated with battling glossophobia. I wasn't ready for failure and I didn't want to do anything too difficult. The fact that I had an issue with being surrounded by speakers better than me, and that I wasn't jumping at the opportunity to be mentored by those speakers, goes to show just how mentally unprepared I was to succeed.

The fact that I couldn't join in the fun and just laugh at that guy's jokes showed that I was secretly hoping other speakers would fail and the crowd would think they sucked so I wouldn't look so bad when I went up there. Lastly, my failure to realize that in order to overcome the fear of public speaking, I had to speak, showed that I had no clue what I was doing.

Once you decide you are ready to overcome your fear, these quirks don't matter. The fact is, Toastmasters is cheap, accessible for even the busiest of people, and it's a great platform to use to make strides towards your goal. When you're looking to be in front of an audience, your well of speaking opportunities may run dry before you get your fear to the level you want. Unless I get my act together and follow through with my plan to start Scared Speechless Clubs, there isn't really another affordable, convenient, and widely available option for giving speeches on a consistent basis.

So, before joining Toastmasters, keep in mind that every club is different. You may feel intimidated, out of sorts, deathly afraid—you may even feel as if you're at an eighteenth century Prime Ministerial dinner reception, and you're the only guest from the modern day. Regardless of this and any other oddities you may encounter, as noted—and it can't be stressed enough—one of the most important ways to overcome your fear is to put yourself outside your comfort zone, preferably via speeches, on a consistent basis. Regardless of the club you decide to join, Toastmasters will serve that purpose. So, get ready for some awkward standing ovations, Toastmaster!

CHAPTER 22:

Roadblocks I Faced That You'll Face Too

"But after a moment of temporary discomfort, I took a deep breath, scanned the room, and asked myself…what's the absolute worst that can happen?"

— ME, an important question I ask myself often

E ven with a never-give-up mentality, a killer action plan, and the motivation to excel, there could still be times where you'll lose hope. I had an awful time with the third set of tasks on my list. My fear level before volunteering to conduct a prepared presentation at work went from my initially reported 7.5 to about a 9. I was officially panicking.

What if everyone thinks I'm weird? Or, what if they think I'm a know-it-all for trying to present in this work meeting? What if my boss takes offense to me even asking? What the hell will I do if he says no?

Bertha had always driven me up the wall with this. Though I'd known there was nothing that would kick me off my path, she had kept trying to plant the seed in my mind that all of this effort wasn't worth it. After all, it was entirely possible that I'd do these things and quit before seeing any notable improvements. But as you have seen, I shook off the doubt, pushed forth, and proved her wrong.

The same thing had occurred the second time I was set to volunteer to present at work. Even though the first time went relatively well, I still hadn't found that comfort zone so I was going at it a second time. On that occasion, I'd been going to present to a larger group. My fear had hit damn close to a 9.0 again, and I'd considered replacing that task with something a little less risky.

What if I say something stupid and lose my job?

Just as I'd started to spiral down into the abyss of worst possible "what-if" scenarios, I controlled myself, remembered *The Pact* I'd made, and started to think more clearly. Besides, I knew that this terrible feeling was nothing compared to what I'd feel if I quit now. As panic subsided and reality set in, I realized this wasn't the big deal I'd made it out to be.

Approaching my second work presentation, I felt like I was awaiting impending death by firing squad. Butterflies were wreaking havoc in my stomach. I walked to the middle of the room, smiling, not smiling, looking at my notecard, scratching my leg, itching my ear, and moving my feet like a high school nerd dancing alone to nineties hip-hop.

But after a moment of temporary discomfort, I took a deep breath, scanned the room, and said to myself: *What's the absolute worst that can happen? Maybe I'll say something dumb and I'll have to regain my colleagues' confidence. This is no big deal. I got this.*

I finished my presentation and took a seat—drenched in sweat, ears ringing, hands freezing cold—but I felt amazing. I had grappled with fear and emerged victorious!

The next work topic presentation wasn't preceded by panic, rather, I was beset by a weird mix of extreme nervousness and excitement. My heart raced, my palms trembled, my voice shook—but I wasn't terrified. I'd harnessed the elation I'd felt after the last time I'd faced my fear and conquered it.

The fourth time was another step in the right direction. By the fifth, I was cracking jokes, teaching lessons, and feeling like a total stud.

Given my newfound comfort with work presentations, I thought I'd finally learned to manage fear. But contrary to my hopes, it wasn't over yet. When I moved on to the next set of tasks that involved presentations, I started feeling similar symptoms: all the horrible things that could happen clouded my mind, my voice trembled, my hands grabbed at places they shouldn't be grabbing at in public—I felt it all. The spontaneous speeches were even more terrifying: *I'm about to talk about something I don't know much about with no chance to prepare? Shoot me now.*

The gnawing in my stomach was almost unbearable. But this time, my doubts weren't as dismal—my recent accomplishments had diminished them. This shift in concentration allowed me to work on improving my presentation—things like the quality of my material, injecting humor, telling interesting stories, and improving my audience interaction. Even though I still got nervous, my only concern became giving good speeches, not figuring out how to get out of them.

Additional Fear-Strangling Tips

When you have a piece of paper in front of you with everything you need to do to achieve your goals, it's easy to get tunnel vision. So, keep in mind that it's important to jump on every opportunity to push your limits, whether or not it's on your list. One strategy I employed to get over a lot of my social phobias—and in turn, to help with my public speaking—was doing things that I wouldn't normally do because they would embarrass me.

Allow me to explain. When I was an eager, soon-to-be college graduate, I'd attend industry networking events. This is how a typical night would unfold:

7:35-7:55 PM:	Pre-game in car to loosen up a bit.
8:00 PM:	Enter event wearing nice new suit, feeling fresh and confident.
8:00-8:15 PM:	Walk around scoping out targets I wanted to approach. Make a lot of model-like facial and body gestures while maintaining abnormally erect posture.
8:15-8:45 PM:	Finish initial walkthrough. Stand in corner to think of action plan.
8:45-8:50 PM:	Make final decision on targets I wanted to approach.
8:50-9:00 PM:	Wait in line to purchase a shot. Take shot, gag, go back to planning corner.
9:00-9:20 PM:	Brainstorm strategy for approach.
9:20-9:40 PM:	Pump myself up. Whisper things like, "I just gotta do it!" and "YOLO!"
9:40-10:30 PM:	Continue whispering positive things to myself.

10:30-10:55 PM: Wait in line for a beer. Talk to disinterested bartender about global warming.

10:55 PM: Turn around and realize the people I wanted to talk to have left.

10:55-11:05 PM: Feel terrible about missing out on a great opportunity.

11:05-11:15 PM: Make second walk around, scoping out targets I wanted to approach.

11:16 PM: Come to stark realization: "I'm in a den of unemployed fools."

11:20 PM: Leave, go to Denny's*.

Some may argue that social anxiety has little to do with fear of public speaking, but for me, it did. My public speaking fears affected my confidence because of a shattered self-view. I constantly hesitated in social and professional networking situations. Gaining confidence with public speaking has drastically improved my ability to interact socially—and as a result, I've gained even more power over my doubts.

After deciding to do whatever was necessary to overcome my fear, the networking event bomb was no longer acceptable. The next time I went, this is what that same networking event looked like:

8:00 PM: Enter event wearing nice new suit, feeling confident.

8:00-8:15 PM: Walk around, find someone I wanted to approach. Close my eyes, count to three, walk up to them to introduce myself.

8:15-8:45 PM: Have an awesome conversation. Exchange information. Excuse myself.

8:50 PM:	Have a quick look around, find second person I want to talk to. Count to three, make approach.
8:50-9:00 PM:	Have a subpar conversation, exchange information, and move on. Make a few quick mental notes on what went wrong and how to avoid it happening again.
9:00-10:30 PM:	Apply lessons learned, walk around talking to anyone and everyone, making a bunch of cool new contacts.
10:30-10:45 PM:	Get a drink, kick back, laugh about ever feeling scared in these situations.
10:45 PM:	Leave networking event.
11:00-12:00 PM:	Arrive home, watch an episode of my favorite show, go to sleep completely satisfied.

I've come a long way from walking around aimlessly, too scared to talk to anyone for four hours, ending the night with a tear-drenched Denny's appetizer sampler.

How you go about doing this is up to you. Maybe you don't like to go out to bars or you don't feel a need to go to networking events. But it's important to stop at various times throughout the day and think, "What can I do right now that would normally make me shrivel up like a prune?"

This isn't a cure for public speaking anxiety on its own, and neither is the formula I presented in previous chapters. The reality is that what you do is only twenty percent of the battle. You can give thirty speeches a month, talk to every person at the bar, pester every professional you admire, and do everything in your power to make yourself feel vulnerable. You could dance in front of a thousand sexy people of the opposite gender in a terrifying attempt to woo one of them. You can do whatever you want, really, but what matters more than anything is what's going on in that soft and squishy blob we call a brain. So, when you're progressing through your Plan, know that the struggle will all be worth it.

PART 5

BECOMING AN EFFECTIVE SPEAKER

Note: This section contains quick-fire suggestions and stories to help you get on the road to public speaking excellence. Most of the tips come from my own experiences, failures, and successes. There's a lot of information—read it slowly and pick just a few tips to adopt for each presentation you give. Don't rush to implement all of the recommendations at once, you'll overwhelm yourself.

CHAPTER 23

Speeches 101 – Setting the Tone

"I started researching presentation techniques such as looking just above the eyeline of the spectators, deep breathing exercises, and imagining that the entire audience is naked. I won't tell you which strategy I'm using today, but I will say that you all look REALLY good out there."

— Roy Rosell, from my commencement speech

You can approach a podium with excitement or hopefulness—or you can approach with dread or despair. You can stand with palms soft and open, or with fists clenched and palms drenched. Approach it in whatever way works for you, but NEVER approach a podium without maximum effort—because the more present you are, the better you will perform and the more your audience will love you. And, the more the audience loves you, the more confident and happy you'll feel.

We all have the ability to conduct captivating presentations, but many of us don't ever get to that level. Often, as I noted earlier, that's because we tend to focus on ourselves instead of focusing on our audience. When we're caught up in the terror of giving a speech, we're flooded with thoughts like: *What will go wrong?* and *What can I do to appear calm?* Your audience is not included in that thought process. So, keep your audience at the front of your mind, and remember, being bland, reciting facts, and repressing yourself onstage is not the cure for humiliation. The cure for humiliation is being exceptional.

In 1973, John E. Ware (Southern Illinois School of Medicine), Donald H. Naftulin (University of Southern California School of Medicine), and Frank A. Donnelly (University of Southern California) conducted a fascinating experiment to find out whether a strong delivery technique could so completely bamboozle a group of experts that they overlooked the fact that the content was baloney.

The researchers hired an actor and gave him the fictional identity of "Dr. Fox." He was tasked with presenting a paper titled, "Mathematical Game Theory as Applied to Physician Education." The actor knew nothing of the topic and was directed to work up a lecture full of imprecise waffle, to cite non-existent research papers, and to misstate a lot of information. To succeed at convincing groups of experts that he was the real deal, the actor who played Dr. Fox did one simple thing that many of us fail do time and time again: he appeared to enjoy presenting, and he created the illusion that he was worth listening to. He may not have known anything about the subject he was presenting on, but he had "the look" and "the tone" and he presented confidently.

Dr. Fox's talk was given to three different groups. Groups one and two consisted of mental health educators, while the third group were educators and administrators enrolled in graduate level studies. Just as glossophobes often worry that they might say something wrong and get exposed by the audience, the actor that played Dr. Fox feared that he wouldn't make it through the talk without being uncovered by the experts he was presenting to. Considering that his talk was just a compilation of nonsense, his worries were warranted.

Following the talk, the audience of academics and professionals were asked seven questions regarding Dr. Fox's presentation. Following are the results of that survey:

Questions	Percent that agreed		
	T1	T2	T3
Did he dwell upon the obvious?	50	0	28
Did he seem interested?	100	91	97
Did he use enough examples?	90	64	91
Did he present in well-organized form?	90	82	70
Did he stimulate your thinking?	100	91	87
Did he put his material across in an interesting way?	90	82	81
Have you read any of his publications?	0	9	0

One of the things we can take away from the Dr. Fox experiment is that a speaker has two responsibilities: The first is to satisfy—the audience must feel intrigued, entertained, and connected to your talk. The second is that a speaker should teach the audience something. The actor achieved the first of these and did it so well that he made his audience believe that they were learning something when in fact, they were being fed nonsense. Had he approached the presentation dressed plainly, using a dreary tone, while at the same time presenting real scientific facts, it is likely the feedback for his presentation would have been poor.

So, how can we become effective speakers? Perception, as "Dr. Fox" proved, is critical—the way you present the content and the way you present yourself will make a big difference in your ability to inspire an audience. Content is important too—with words we have the power to educate, inspire, and change people's lives. But how can we maintain an audience's attention for the duration of a talk? How can we truly inspire them, get them emotionally invested in our presentations, and leave them in awe?

There are three things every speech you conduct should contain:

1. *Ethos*: A lot of us are naturally scatterbrained: while watching presentations, we're tempted to scroll through Instagram, swipe through some dating app, or visualize what we'll be doing this weekend. To minimize the chances that your audience will do these things, prove you're worthy of their undivided attention. I'm by no means an expert in any of the topics I've presented on, but in every presentation, I give the audience a reason to listen to me—in other words, I make myself *credible*. Rather than listing your qualifications, be effective—give the audience interesting, compelling stories that relate to your presentation topic.

2. *Logos*: If you have a weak logos—that is, if you don't make sense— your audience will be thinking: "I'm lost," "How did he come to that conclusion?" and "Ehhh, I'll stick to my own beliefs." If your

presentation is hard to follow, or your arguments are unconvincing, your audience will find it easy to dismiss your ideas. Improve your *logos*: back yourself up with facts, statistics, and examples to strengthen your presentation.

3. *Pathos*: Pathos is what makes your speech extraordinary. Every speech is an opportunity to shine and an effective pathos will make your audience love you and feel connected to you. Even better, when an audience feels connected to you emotionally, they'll retain the information you present. Oddly enough, the pathos factor is the one most speakers skip over when they are presenting. They build strong, professional presentations with great information and excellent examples, but they fail to be vulnerable. They fail to show their passion. Consequently, they fail to make an impact.

In our instant-gratification world, where alternative sources of entertainment and information are available at the swipe of a screen, it takes more than a good script to captivate an audience. So, use a strong *ethos*, *logos* and—most importantly—*pathos* to create a solid foundation for your presentation, and then just remember to avoid the common pitfalls of a bad speech! Ask yourself what things will make your audience eager to listen to you—and then include them in your presentation. If you don't, their minds will be heading back to their Tinder apps quicker than you can say, "Wait! I have something interesting to say!"

To help you avoid staring out an audience of web-surfers, in the next chapter we'll cover some of the presentation-killing mistakes that speakers commit. And once you discover what they are, make damn sure you never do them!

CHAPTER 24:

Tips From the Experts –
Why They Fail to Work

Buddy: *"Roy, you keep telling me about all these books you read, and telling me these awesome motivational quotes, but I never see you adopt the things you're telling me. Why?"*

Me: *"That's a great question."*

Buddy: *"Yes. What's the answer?"*

Me: *"If you're committed to changing your life, you'll work hard to make it happen. If...."*

Buddy: *"Damn it, you're doing it again!"*

Note: This chapter aims to bring to light the disconnect between the obsession with self-help books and our dire inability to actually help ourselves. To explain why so many of us fail to "live" the lessons we gather from self-help books, I will revisit concepts shared throughout Part 2 of this book.

L
eading up to and during my freshman year of college, when I overdosed on public speaking literature, I consumed so much content that I started to sound like a living, breathing, self-help book. Any time a friend would complain about how hard one of their classes was, I'd eloquently respond with something cliché like, "Ah, but success does not arrive upon your doorstep without an invitation. Success is a byproduct of resilience! Work longer, harder, and smarter to achieve your goals. It is only then that success will ring your doorbell, compatriot!" When my brother Pablo would feel like quitting his job because his boss was too mean, I'd bring the motivational fire with, "Brother, come hither… the path to greatness is littered with trials and tribulations. You must find your motivation, and allow it to light your path to success! Your boss is only a challenge that you must learn to overcome. Onward, brother!"

I became a purveyor of generic self-help book quotes, launching wisdom bombs to anyone who went so far as to complain, "I'm tired." Because of this, a lot of people started avoiding me like the plague, while others gathered to dump their problems on me. In spewing out this insight, I realized it all started to sound the same—just like the advice in all the public speaking self-help books I was reading at the time seemed to repeat itself. I asked myself: *How do these authors get away with restating the same information already revealed in hundreds of other books*? I concluded that they gathered in bi-monthly meetings to decide the next wave of self-help literature:

Best-selling self-help author #1: Oh…My…God…Eureka! I've discovered the key to success! It's fish oil! I need to tell the world about this ASAP!

Best-selling self-help author #2: Not so fast, pal. I discovered that eons ago. I've already written half the book. It's getting published in Q4 this year.

Best-selling self-help author #1: Shut up, idiot! Stop trying to take credit for all my revolutionary ideas!

Best-selling self-help author #3: Damn it! I've always wanted to write a book about fish oil! Now what will I write about...Acai? The power of yogurt? Kombucha?! I'm doomed!

Mediator: Settle down, people. Why don't you BOTH write about fish oil and we'll design cool dust covers and catch phrases so they all feel different?

Best-selling self-help authors: *Joyful dances and celebrations.*

Contrary to what my frustrations at the time made me believe, today I know that such meetings do not occur. The reason experts preach about the same concepts and strategies is because these things have been proven to work. We've heard the 'how to overcome fear' lessons many times and we know that they work. So, why do most people still crumble when giving a speech? And why isn't everyone a fear-killing machine?

For one, many of us don't consume advice with the intention of taking action. Do you think I was really implementing all the advice I was spewing to anyone who confided their issues with me? Nope...we consume advice, filter out the "too much work to implement" advice, then take action on the rest. We digest the information, then split the recommendations into three categories:

1. What we will do: The action items we decide are easy enough to achieve now. For me, this included things like "practice more," "do deep breathing exercises," and "rehearse in front of a mirror."

2. What we might do: This is the stuff we've got to do some work for. If we find the time, the energy, the resources, the perfect moment...then we'll do this. Recommendations like "practice in front of your friends and family" and "join a speech class" fall in to this category.

3. What we'll skip: This stuff requires us to work our butts off. Towards the end of my struggle, I pushed myself on most things, but for many, I convinced myself that I didn't have the time, energy, or resources to accomplish them. This included recommendations that asked me to do something that terrified me, like "present in front of co-workers" or "sing in front of a group."

Ask yourself: How many times have you heard great advice, felt motivated to try it out, but never got around to it? Additionally, how often do you give advice that you haven't adopted yourself? We are inundated with great motivational quotes and life lessons from social media, books, and people who have achieved exactly what we're aiming to achieve. But how often do we implement the lessons, instead of just hitting *retweet*?

It's the things we skip that result in the most progress, while the things we act on are supplemental to the tasks in the other two categories above. In my glossophobia-busting journey, I did the majority of things the experts were recommending—I even tried doing stuff outside my comfort zone, but I still wasn't seeing the progress they promised. Those recommendations were:

1. Know you are in the majority

2. Tackle your fear head on

3. Know your material

4. Know your audience

5. Be yourself

6. Relax

7. Mistakes are okay.

That's the seven-line recap for virtually every public speaking book, video, or article you'll encounter. Within each of these seven pieces of advice, there are action items to achieve. Conceptually speaking, these lessons make a lot of sense, and, if applied correctly, they work. It is in the *application* of these concepts that most of us crash and burn. Let's look at these steps one by one....

You are in the majority

On the first day of my Freshman Political Science class, five students were set to present. I was scheduled to be the fifth presenter, so at the start of class, I scanned the room, searching for the other four presenters. All nerds—skinny, socially awkward, trembling nerds.

I watched nervously as the first presenter, a scrawny little kid with thick-rimmed glasses, wearing a polo shirt about three sizes too large, dragged himself up to the stage, reviewing his notes one last time before his almost-certain doom at the podium. As he reached the front of the room, rustling through his papers, I stared at him intently. I liked the guy, and I wanted him to do well. But I knew that if he fumbled and choked through his speech, I would feel a lot better about presenting after him.

"Hello, class. My name is Michael and today I will be discussing the future of global currency and its impact on the American economy." He beamed. Confidence. Poise. Charisma. Total command over the subject. I watched the remainder of his speech with my jaw on my chest.

When something like this happens, it changes "you are in the majority" from a reassuring notion to something that can make you feel hopeless. But we're looking at it the wrong way. We keep searching for ways to reaffirm that we are in the majority, wasting our energy on an endless quest for self-assurance. But this will only drive us loco. It is difficult to pinpoint who is terrified and who is comfortable, because we all have our methods of disguising our discomfort.

So, instead of trying to confirm that your co-worker Craig or classmate Juan are feeling just as terrible as you are about presenting, save yourself the stress and just treat it as a given. Then, it shouldn't matter as much how great the presentation before yours was. Instead of intimidating you, it could show you that you can be wildly anxious and still conduct a fantastic presentation.

Tackle fear head on

Unless you're wearing protective head gear that's screwed on just right, tackling your fear head on could cause trauma. It's like asking someone out on a date for the first time. One day you decide, "You know what, I could get this girl!" You walk up to her, get rejected, and spend the next month disillusioned. After a while, you're ready to give crush number two a go. Rejection, repeat feelings of dismay. So, what happens next? Either it's going to get progressively easier after consistent failures and lessons learned, or you're going to be at high risk of having self-esteem issues.

For many, tackling the Fear-Controlling Formula I present in Part 4 without first preparing mentally could result in *giving up*. So, if you're going to tackle your fear head on, strengthen your head first. The best way to do this is to turn every failure into a lesson, every butterfly fluttering in your stomach into the impetus to push forward, and every speech into a step up on the ladder to public speaking ease.

Know your material

There's a big difference between knowing your material and being prepared for a presentation. You could have every word of your speech memorized, but still be unprepared. If you don't know how to handle a digital malfunction, recover from a brain fart, or deal with a disinterested audience, you'll end up looking as bad as the guy who forgot he had a speech to do and is forced to improvise. Being prepared means knowing what you're going to say, how you're going to say it, and having a recovery plan when things don't go as envisioned.

For the sake of preserving sanity, ignore the oft-touted advice that you must practice your speech over and over to infinity to become an expert on your subject. Our brains function best when we engage in effective preparation, as discussed in Chapter 12 in the "Taming Fear Through Effective Preparation" section. Effective preparation is eliminating the time spent on speech killers like the pursuit of mastery and script memorization. Instead, focus on understanding the flow of your speech, picking interesting content, and having a "Plan B" in case you lose your place. Then, look through it all and ask: "Would I enjoy this presentation if someone were presenting it to me?" "Would I learn something useful?" If the answer to either question is "No," jump back in. Spice it up a bit. And, always remember: mistakes are human—every member of your audience has royally screwed up a speech at some point, so they get it. Perfection is boring.

Know your audience

Public speaking professionals suggest that arriving early on the day of a presentation to get a feel for the room is a great way to overcome stage anxiety. This is good advice, but the opportunity to interact with your audience before a presentation isn't always possible, particularly at work or school. So, what happens when you hear that it's imperative to get to know your audience before speeches but you can't always do it? You'll feel like you've been short-handed and, even if you've practiced like a madman and can outclass Dr. Phil in a debate of who's the most knowledgeable of know-it-alls, you'll start to feel panicked.

The truth is, you know your workplace and classroom audience because you've been in it before. You know your audience because you *are* the audience and even if you haven't met each member personally, it's fine—you don't need to. Things like not being able to follow through with a preparation "requirement" like this won't doom your speech—unless you believe it will.

Be yourself

Throughout the twelve years I lived with glossophobia, I was inundated with suggestions like, "Be you, man!" and, "Be yourself and they'll listen!" I always discarded these recommendations in my mind's trash bin because more often than not, because of my fear of public speaking and social anxiety, I wasn't yet the person I wanted to be.

Public speaking is a performance—one that allows you to become the person you're striving to become. If you're still striving to become the ideal version of yourself, try being the person you want to be when you're on stage. A presentation is your chance to break out of your shell and let your potential take the reins. If your lifelong dream is to become a marketing executive but you're a server at the local Olive Garden˚, then talk like the marketing executive you want to be and force that room to see you in a different light. Don't discard what makes you. Don't be afraid to throw in some "future you."

Relax

Telling a glossophobe to relax is like telling your wife to take a few deep breaths after you accidentally left your three-year-old at the park. A glossophobe won't hear "You just need to relax!" and suddenly have this revelatory experience like "My God! I can't believe I didn't realize this sooner! All I had to do was relax!" The truth is, you don't need to relax to succeed at getting comfortable with public speaking. (But you do need to make sure you didn't leave your three-year-old at the park.)

There may be a few activities that will reduce your pre-presentation anxiety, such as stretching, deep breathing, doing an intense gym workout, doing an extra run-through of your speech, or taking shots. But instead of expending all your effort trying to settle your heartbeat, try harnessing that fear, use it to your advantage. Accept that your heartbeat will quicken before a speech, your stomach will tighten, and you'll feel nervous. There's no point trying to eliminate fear; your time is better spent redefining it as *excitement*.

When I present and start to feel that nervous tension, I treat it as a motivational boost, a signal telling me that what I'm about to do is going to make me stronger.

Mistakes are okay

Tell this to the kid who blanked on stage and is in a bathroom stall puking his brains out. Of course, errors are okay. We learn from mistakes; they make us stronger—we've all heard the spiel. But don't say that to someone who just screwed up royally and is scared beyond reason of making a mistake again. It's not comforting.

For most people, the fear of public speaking is not a fear of speaking itself. We don't fear talking to a group of people—we fear the terrible way talking to a group of people makes us *feel*. So, we have a problem accepting that mistakes are okay. The realization that screwing up isn't as bad as we've made ourselves believe it is doesn't come from being told by an expert in a book. It comes from exposure to failure.

And when I'm talking about failure, I'm not just referring to public speaking failure—I'm talking about all types of failures in life. For example, I spent years failing like a flailing drunk trying to find a date outside a Miami club. Why was I so scared? I researched, I pondered, slammed my head against walls trying to figure out why I couldn't control my fear. With each crushing failure, I would dust myself off, walk right back up to that swanky club—and fail again. I was being persistent as all the books suggested, why wasn't it getting easier? Well, because like many glossophobes, I was overlooking the lessons each of my failures was trying to teach me.

When you treat each failure as a lesson, and you redefine the role of your failure, you'll be well on your way to achieving whatever you've set your mind on. I did it by standing in front of 15,000 people at my university's graduation ceremony, taking a deep breath, and conducting a speech—a speech in which every word seemed to flow from my heart to my mouth—no Bertha to tear me down, no insecurity. For the first time since fifth grade, I wasn't insecure about my image, self-conscious about the tremble in my voice, or obsessed about what the audience thought of me. That day, I stood in a place where I was so accustomed to feeling dread, and for the first time in more than a decade, I felt at home in front of an audience.

During my seemingly endless fight with glossophobia, my priority wasn't to make a career of public speaking—it was to be able to speak to an audience without almost projectile vomiting every time. I didn't need to be a champion speaker or the reincarnation of Abraham Lincoln. I just wanted to stop being a wimp, and I wanted my audience to have a good time. But because the self-help books I read were written by people who were masters in their fields, I lost interest in them—I just couldn't relate. It took defining the lessons on my own terms for me to digest them. More importantly, I realized this: If you are committed to changing your life, you will work hard to make it happen. If you're not, you'll find an excuse.

CHAPTER 25:

Ten Speaking Crimes Most Speakers Commit

"That's a canine," said the teacher.

"What's a canine?" asked the little girl.

"It's a dog," responded the teacher.

"Well, why didn't you say that in the first place?"

There are lots of things that can make an audience lose interest in what you have to say—and you might already be doing some of them. Is your vocal tone strong or could you put a little more oomph into it? Are you pacing yourself or speeding through your speech? Are you relying heavily on your notes? Is your material bland, or disorganized? All of these things are all fixable—just be aware of what you're doing and aim to improve each one during your talks.

I've been put to sleep by countless speeches in my lifetime, and I know I've induced my share of catnaps as well. So, to help make sure that you do not become the purveyor of one-way tickets to Snoozeville, following is a list of the most common sleep-inducing blunders speakers make. Every time I think of a presenter that did the following things, I just want to ZzZzZzZzZz....

Being too wordy.

There is a common misconception that the more detail you provide in your speech and the more in-depth your examples are, the more intelligent you appear. Because of this misconception, speakers may tend to speak too much, muddy their diction, or explain relatively simple concepts in overcomplicated terminology.

During your presentations, are you dressing up your diction in seventeenth century lace collars and cuffs in order to sound more knowledgeable? Are you looking for fancy replacements for simple words and going into detail explaining topics that need no more than a sentence or two? The next time you're preparing for a speech, ask yourself: "Does my audience really need to know this? Can I say this using less words/slides?"

Being too formal.

With regards to the level of formality expected of an effective orator, it is of vast significance to produce flowing content to target audiences of varying multitudes and distillations. This content need not be exceedingly pompous, for pomposity shall attain naught more than a shambolic assemblage of spectators and may stir in thee sentiments of disdain, both for thyself and thy overly ostentatious manner of articulation.

Don't be a phony—speak like a person—loosen up a bit.

In addition, don't get caught holding a bagful of facts. Facts, research findings, and statistics are all important parts of presentations, but you need to balance them with educated opinion, compelling commentary, and if appropriate, side-splitting humor. Remember: the most important thing isn't the information you're providing; the most important thing is that the audience retains that information. The best way to get them to remember it is to be memorable, so don't be afraid to mix the formality of academic/professional language and examples with some fun.

"Can you all see this?"

In addition to over-crowded presentation slides and the career-busting crime of reading to your audience, there is the scandal of the hard-to-read presentation. Viewing your slide deck shouldn't require that the audience wear corrective lenses, so be wary of using slide color contrasts that are hard to read, and of including unnecessary styles, funky borders, or weird templates on your slides.

Unless you're presenting to hundreds or thousands of people, or your audience is too far back to see the podium—or it's standing-room-only and they're plastered against the sides of the room—you shouldn't need to ask, "Can everyone see this?" If you ever feel inclined to ask this question, chances are you've included too much text in your slides or you need to restructure your visuals so that everything is clear and concise.

Reading the presentation.

This is arguably the most annoying bad habit of all. And the problem is, if you don't know you're doing it, you'll keep doing it. If you're nervous, feel you're not getting your point across, or forget what you're going to say next, it's tempting to peek at your presentation document and read what's written there. But by doing this, you've just lost your audience.

By reading your slides, you're telling your audience that everything they need to know is already on the screen, so there's no reason to listen to you. To avoid this, make sure each slide includes only key points (or preferably, images) that will help you stay on track. Your slides should look clean, be text-sparse, and contain as much empty space as possible. For the most part, your slides should support the words coming out of your mouth, not repeat them.

You may feel naked and exposed the first couple times you conduct a presentation without the comfort of half your script being behind you, but you'll quickly realize you never really needed it.

Being generic.

If you do exactly what the audience expects, you'll have a disinterested audience. To avoid this, think of five boring speeches you've seen—you don't remember the content of a single one of them, do you? But this will rekindle your memory: the speaker walked to the podium, gave a brief, boring introduction, then ran through their topic. Finally, their "Conclusion" slide looming next to them, they provided a dreary recap of the material you'd already forgotten. Am I right?

Everyone has the power to be unique and original, but one must dare to try.

Put your own personal twist on every presentation. Throw in personal experiences and unique stories to back up your key points. Explain concepts in fresh language instead of using stock examples your audience has heard before.

Getting attention the wrong way.

I witnessed one speech I'll never forget. During a college marketing class, the presenter walked up, looked at the audience, and with a sly smile on his face, screamed, "Bang! Just seeing if everyone's awake!!" Attention-getting? Sure! Obnoxious? Absolutely! Annoying? Incredibly! I guess this guy had been reading way too many "start your presentation with a bang!" articles. Had he used this introduction to open a presentation about the Samsung Note 7, it might have worked. But the presentation was about financial planning, so it made no sense. Don't use cheap, unimaginative tricks when trying to get your audience's attention. Instead, think of clever, creative ways that are related to your topic to draw your audience in from the get-go.

One good example of this would be a tactic used during a pitch my former business partner and I conducted at a start-up competition about a year after graduating from university. We were pitching a service that would help high-achieving students get their information on the hiring manager's desk, thus bypassing the "black hole" that resumes usually end up in. To start the presentation, my partner and I walked up to the stage and without saying a word, we each raised a stack of about 300 papers above our heads and dropped them on the floor. The audience was stunned. "This is the stack of resumes applicants submitted for that internship you just applied to," I said. The audience was hooked.

Using filler words.

We use filler words to hold our place in a conversation—partly out of habit, partly because we're afraid of transitional silence. But as famed English actor Sir Ralph Richardson once said, "The most precious things in speech are the pauses." Nothing hinders your credibility quicker than the overuse of filler words. If you're not sure if you use filler words, you do. Don't believe it? Have someone film you speaking or ask a friend to keep count during your next presentation. I'm not saying you need to slap yourself every time you say "uh," nor am I suggesting you should dedicate yourself to eliminating filler words. But if one or more of the following words makes up more than ten percent of your presentations, then you have work to do.

- You know?   - Like
- Basically   - Actually
- Supposedly   - Totally
- Literally   - Honestly

- Personally   - Seriously

- Okay, so...   - Pretty much

- I mean   - Um

- Uhhh   - Emmm

These flow disruptors communicate *doubt*. When overused, they force the audience to dig to find the meaning behind your words. If your audience has to put effort into figuring out what you're saying, many will decide it's not worth the work.

Okay so, pretty much...if you, like, use filler words a lot, ummm, basically you...uh… should work on that. You know?

Not looking at the audience.

Your audience doesn't consist of shiny, sun-reflecting objects that will blind you if you face them. Your family will not be hounded by a mob of demon children if you look at the audience (however, those creepy posts on social media warning you to forward to ten friends or a ghost will rip out your eyeballs in the middle of the night are another story—I'll never stop forwarding those). For the most part, the audience is just hoping to be intrigued by your talk.

So, ignore the "fear-reducing" advice you've probably heard about staring at a poster at the back of the room or ogling the chins of audience members to avoid eye contact. Eye contact is powerful. It creates an immediate connection and can even put people on the edge of their seats—just where you want them. They'll feel they're being spoken to directly and they'll pay attention.

Not involving the audience.

Everyone seems to agree that engaging your audience in your speech is a great way to make it more enjoyable, but few professional speakers suggest *how* to do that. Of course, there are countless ways to include your audience in your presentation—you can ask for a show of hands or ask for volunteers to help you out with interactive tasks. But the best way to involve your audience? *Play with their emotions.* Make them feel like they're part of your presentation by using audience-inclusive stories to demonstrate points. Use hypothetical situations and include audience members as examples. Instead of throwing facts at them, use Barbara the accountant in the front row or Brett the hot-shot manager at the back of the room to make your point (but don't poke fun or make Barb or Brett feel bad). Make your audience feel like the protagonists in your presentation and they'll feel connected—to you and to your talk.

Additionally, try putting faces on ideas to engage audience members emotionally. Turn 'I' or 'he' in your story into 'we' and 'you.' Use metaphors and analogies of experiences that everyone shares to help explain new concepts. Try to make your presentations feel more like conversations than lectures.

Failing to display excitement.

The listener has to feel that the presenter is feeling great, even if he (or she) isn't. You have to exude confidence and radiate feel-good vibes. Speakers must jump-start themselves at the moment of performance no less than actors, dancers, and musicians do. If you are emanating an "I don't want to be here" vibe and you back it up with a tired tone, lackluster gestures, and monotonous material, your audience will be bored stiff.

And, if you're a nervous wreck on stage and tend to cover by trying to appear calm, chances are you look bored. Whenever you present to an audience, have fun. Don't take yourself so seriously! Find the parts of your talk that you feel passionate about and SHOW that passion. Let the audience know that what you're saying is interesting and important, through your tone, gestures, and actions. By doing this, not only will you release some of the tension you're feeling, you'll get the audience engrossed and excited.

Now, that's the stuff that standing ovations and "Come-back-and-speak-to-us-again-soon" invitations are made of!

CHAPTER 26:

Ten Easy Fixes to Become a Great Speaker

"Talent is cheaper than table salt. What separates the talented individual from the successful one is a lot of hard work."

—STEPHEN KING, legendary horror writer

As you have seen, I've spent thousands of hours trying desperately to figure out ways to lessen my public speaking anxiety. That didn't leave much time to spend on becoming a better public speaker. Instead of studying how to develop an engaging vocal tone, I focused on concealing the tremor in my voice. Instead of researching ways to integrate humor into my presentations, I was fixated on playing it safe to avoid ridicule. Yes, I eventually learned to love public speaking, but I had to work hard to become a speaker worth listening to.

After overcoming my fear, my journey to becoming a fun-to-watch, magnetic speaker began. While fishing for ways to get better and better, I learned that the riskiest strategy when presenting is to be restrained. I did it all my life in feeble—and failed—attempts to conceal my fear. It wasn't until I controlled my fear that I realized how much holding back during presentations has ruined speeches with great potential. Good speakers are aware of this, and they constantly innovate their talks to make them entertaining and informative. I hope you'll try the following strategies to get a little better every time you speak.

Show Your Passion.

This is the most important factor—it is what separates a good speech from a great speech. Just as I mentioned in the section on *pathos*, a speaker's passion does wonders to keep an audience enthralled. A speaker can have phenomenal technique, attractive charts, and an intriguing message, but it's passion that makes an audience feel emotionally connected. Passion is contagious. Speakers who display passion are often seen as the best speakers, even if they may be a step behind technically—and even if they aren't experts in their field. Remember "Dr. Fox?"

That said, it's important not to confuse passion with performance. You may have heard suggestions like "Bring emotion into your talk—show them you care!" and "Smile, use body gestures, speak confidently—they'll see your passion!" Though a more "active" presentation will naturally increase the attention levels of your audience, it isn't as easy to show passion as it is to make technical changes to a presentation. But, exuding passion is key to a successful presentation—you can't expect to inspire and influence others if you're not feeling inspired.

"But, Roy," you might be thinking, "I have to conduct a presentation about budgeting to my department at work. I can't stand talking about money. In fact, I hate my job. How can I be passionate?"

When you're faced with a subject you feel absolutely no passion towards, don't fret: however mundane your topic may be, there's always a way to add zing. If you have to talk about saving money, talk about the piggy bank your mom made you put coins in when you were young and how, years later, you got her a beautiful gift with the money you saved. Talk about the time you overspent and couldn't take your kids to the waterpark like you promised. Talk about anything that brings you genuine emotions of happiness, sadness, anxiety, nostalgia—whatever gives your words purpose—and *pathos*. Your audience will feel your passion and be drawn into your emotional world.

Watch yourself and get honest feedback.

It took watching footage of my speeches to committing all the sleep-inducing blunders listed in the previous chapter. I looked at my slides sixty percent of the time, stared down at my note cards twenty percent of the time, and scanned the audience awkwardly the rest of the time. My vocal tone was colorless, my body was rigid, and I stood behind the safety of a table for entire presentations. I tried too hard to sound smart and composed. As a result, I looked and sounded bored—and I bored everyone in the room.

Every time I'd ask people what they thought of a speech, I'd get a flurry of generic responses ("Great job!" and "Pretty good!") and a few honest responses ("I almost fell asleep, man"). I learned to ignore the generic comments and to concentrate instead on picking out the little gems of feedback people gave about what I might have done better. As I noted earlier, get a friend or family member to film your presentations, and then have your whole clan watch the recording and give you honest, *constructive criticism*. What can you improve? What works? What doesn't? Then, implement the suggestions you agree with. Get into the habit of analyzing what you did right, where you could have done better, and dedicate yourself to improving after every speech.

Ask "What's in It for Me?"

I've come to realize that some people are perpetually so distracted, they'd be more intrigued by standing in a desolate parking lot catching Pokémon on their cell phones than by listening to a speech revealing the location of the Holy Grail. Aim to answer this question for your audience: "What's in it for me?" Why is what you have to offer better than scrolling through Instagram? In the age of unlimited distractions, before they decide to keep their attention on you, an audience must know what you bring to the table. So, as you're preparing your speech, remember that "What's in it for me?" is key—review your logos, ethos, and pathos. Is it strong enough to answer that question?

Keep in mind that you'll usually have a couple of know-it-alls in your audience who will dis you regardless of what you offer. Don't sweat the small stuff—most of the audience is rooting for you so put yourself in their shoes and ask, "What would make me want to pay attention to this speaker?" Go from there.

Start strong.

When researching powerful ways to start your speeches, before you decide to implement the advice you find online or elsewhere, ask yourself, "How many people have read/seen this?" Then ask, "Should I replicate something my audience has probably seen?"

Presentation openers are like conversation starters. You have only a few seconds to make a positive impression. Even if you're a high school dropout with no job, no prospects, and a history of failed relationships, you can attract someone's attention based upon how you utilize those first twenty or so seconds. Sell yourself! If you start a conversation with a stock pickup line, you'll probably lose the other person's attention right off the bat. If you take too long to make your value proposition (what benefits the listener will get from listening to you), the person(s) you are speaking to will be itching to get away. So, even if your topic of discussion is something as mind-blowingly mundane as eighteenth century knitting techniques, you can still enthrall your audience with a good introduction. Instead of just leading with, "Have you ever wondered how people made clothes in the eighteenth century?" you can follow up with, "I know what you're thinking: eighteenth-century knitting techniques? Just kill me now!" Then, make a direct connection to draw the person you're speaking to into the conversation. "Did you know that the beanie you're wearing is a throwback to hats knitted by eighteenth century Scottish bonnet makers using hand-hewn wooden needles?" No subject is boring if you approach it with a willingness to take risks.

Avoid information overload.

If you have a bunch of topics you want to cover, but can't figure out a way to fit it all in in a coherent and organized way, you risk losing your audience to information overload. I've fallen victim to this peril several times, especially when presenting on a topic I'm passionate about (such as soccer—or overcoming fear).

This is also the case for broad topics like "The 1960s," "Marketing," or "Modern Fashion." If you try to cover broad topics in one presentation, chances are you'll end up being all over the place. You simply can't cover every aspect of any of these topics in a reasonable amount of time. Instead, find an interesting topic niche. Instead of "The 1960s," for example, try "The Los Angeles Cocaine Epidemic of the 60s." Instead of Marketing, try "Digital Marketing to Teenage Girls." Instead of "Modern Fashion," try "How to Be a Successful Pant Model."

Humor 'em!

A fair chunk of the population has no idea that there are people in the world who dedicate their lives to being entertaining. Don't worry about the curmudgeons among us—instead, make the rest of us laugh. A little humor will make a terrible speech tolerable, a mediocre speech good, and a good speech great.

But what will make them laugh? Fart humor? Persistent self-deprecation? Sexual innuendos? These things probably won't get you too far. Humor is achieved through spontaneity. Don't be afraid to depart from the expected. Be innovative, impulsive, and most of all, be you. Use metaphors, comical comparisons, and jokes pertaining to your topic. If you watch my commencement speech (check it out here: https://youtu.be/ aS0_LiSaRIQ), you'll see that I use the joke of comparing my disappointing life to that of a Clippers fan. Considering the speech was given in Los Angeles, this worked great with my audience (best if you don't chuckle awkwardly at your own joke, though).

Script like a boss.

There are instances in which a script is acceptable. This is rare, but if you do find yourself giving a graduation speech or a eulogy, there are three things you can do to make sure your audience doesn't start to feel disconnected.

1. Speak when you're looking up. This will take practice, but it will do you huge favors. Instead of looking down, reading a sentence, then looking up to make eye contact, try looking down, retaining a sentence, and looking up as you speak it. It's a simple trick and it does wonders.

2. Kill the "reading tone." Be loud and be proud. Enunciate your key points so they stick with your audience. In fact, when reading from a script, be dynamic—articulate your main ideas more

forcefully than you would for a script-less speech. When reading, the last thing you want to do is—well—sound like you're reading.

3. Move! Gesticulate! As Muddy Waters would say, "Get your mojo working!" But moving one hand like an orchestra conductor isn't going to cut it. Be excited to be up there and let your passion show. A lack of movement in conjunction with minimal eye contact will result in a disinterested audience. In other words: stiff + shy = stultifying.

Stand out.

"Mr. President, Vice-President, Chancellor, Assistant Chancellor, Dean, Associate Dean, Head of Events, Members of Council, esteemed Representatives of the College of Business, and fellow Graduates." ... *Rest of introduction and body of speech.* ... "I want to thank my parents for teaching me, my brother for being there, my friends for motivating me, my Aunt Jemima for helping me, my boyfriend/girlfriend for inspiring me, and I also want to thank...."

Aside from the Mistress of Syrups being my aunt, how generic was that? Yes, sometimes we must preface a speech with the type of list above, but even in required acknowledgements, aim to be different, for your sake, and for audience enjoyment. We've all heard speeches with long introductions thanking everyone from parents to dogs to third-grade teachers. Welcome to Snoozeville. Avoid corny clichés and old chestnuts—be creative.

Update your speech for each audience.

I have an acquaintance who does motivational speeches regularly. He's a polished presenter—he's lively, he uses powerful gestures, he's passionate about his topics, and he speaks to a wide array of audiences with differing views and interests. So, what's the problem? He uses the same speech each time, with the same jokes and level of audience involvement. Whereas certain one-liners work wonders for a group of under-motivated used-car salesmen, others only work for the Latinos in the audience. Some parts of his speech strike a chord for audience members who grew up in Los Angeles, but completely miss the mark for those who have never been there. The point is, there is no "one size fits all" when it comes to presentations, so adjust your humor, examples, and stories accordingly. As I noted earlier, you don't need to show up three hours before a talk to learn something about every member of your audience. But you do need to understand your audience. Are they urban high school kids? Business professionals? Elementary school teachers? What interests them? What are their values? Prepare your speech from there.

Attempt the Absurd.

As the great Spanish writer Miguel de Cervantes once said, "In order to attain the impossible, one must attempt the absurd." But what he could have said was, "In order to attain _____ (fill in the blank with any goal you wish to achieve), one must attempt the absurd."

271

Most people who give speeches are pursuing the same goal. They want to entertain and be informative—and they want to be liked. They'll scour the web looking for tips on how to do all these things and stumble across the same advice others have already found. Instead of standing out from the masses, they end up doing something that countless others have already tried.

The way around this? Be unique. Don't fixate on standards, protocol, or what is expected of you. Attempt the absurd—take the advice you've gathered, then add your own distinct twist of charm when implementing it.

As the old saying goes, *Be yourself, everyone else is already taken.* You don't need extraordinary confidence to succeed as a speaker. Hell, there are times when I'm feeling insecure, down in the dumps, had a terrible week, but still have to give a speech. When this happens (and even when I'm confident), I find the purpose in every presentation I give. Are you presenting to better the lives of your audience? To promote a product you've put your heart and soul into? To impress your boss for a potential raise? For every speech you give, find your purpose, and rock the socks off that audience with your passion.

CHAPTER 27:

Back to the Beginning

Dad: *Your speech is today, hijo. There gonna be a lot of people there. Joo ready?*

Me: *I think so, Papa.*

Dad: *A lot of people watching joo.*

Me: *Yeah, Papa, that's true.*

Dad: *If joo say something stupid, A LOT of people gonna hear it.*

Me: *Yup, I know.*

Dad: *How many is it? 10,000? 12,000? Imagine if joo messed up....*

Me: *15,000 Papa. Yeah, that would be pretty funny.*

Dad: *I've taught joo well, hijo....*

As I stood at the podium at my Cal Poly Pomona graduation ceremony, crouched over the stand with hunchback-like posture and an ill-fitting cap held down with about a dozen pins, I remembered *Diffendoofer Day*. I thought about the mocking faces of the twenty-five high school kids in the class that day as I'd stood, voiceless, broken, in complete emotional disarray. Then, I recalled the "state of the company" event at NBCUniversal that could have propelled my career to new heights had I just garnered the courage to talk to people, and how hard I'd fought to conjure up the courage to ask a question in front of those couple hundred audience members. I relived the memory of every failed presentation, botched opportunity, and nauseated half hour spent in a bathroom stall—it all came back to me, seconds before the biggest speech I'd ever given.

For most of my life, I'd had a terrorizing fear of public speaking, but there I was, about to fly or flop in front of 15,000 people. As the memories continued to pile up, I couldn't help but smile. I'd been through a lot, but that wasn't me anymore—and for the first time in my life, I couldn't wait to get up there. With that, I adjusted my posture, looked out into the endless sea of black gowns, took a deep breath, and began to speak:

"Upon being notified that I'd been selected to receive this honor, I was absolutely ecstatic. I called my mom, posted my achievement on Facebook and got a ton of likes from people I barely know. It was an exciting five minutes for me. It was the kind of excitement that tops off years of never being quite good enough, of being so close to success yet failing miserably when it mattered most. Kind of like being a Clippers fan.

After those minutes of elation, I managed to settle down a bit. I took a deep breath, picked up the phone and made a call to the College of Business. It was then that I was informed that I'd have to prepare a speech to present in front of approximately 15,000 people. So, let me give you a little background:

All my life, I've been deathly afraid of two things. Public speaking—and spiders. The idea of public speaking horrified me to such an extent that if a professor ever gave one of my classes the option of jumping into a pool filled with venomous water spiders in place of giving a speech, I'd be the first one with my swimming trunks on. But somewhere along the way, I realized something. I realized I couldn't continue to allow this fear to consume me. I started researching presentation techniques such as looking just above the eye line of the spectators, deep breathing exercises and imagining that the entire audience is naked. I won't tell you which strategy I'm using today, but I will say that you all look REALLY good out there.

In a matter of two months, I went from sweating like a madman upon addressing a group of twenty students to conducting persuasive speeches to city councils throughout L.A., to...this. From that moment on, I realized fear is nothing more than a glass barrier waiting to be shattered because it's fear that sets limitations, that makes us complacent, that justifies excuses, that does not allow us to be extraordinary.

Once you've shattered that barrier, there is NOTHING that can stop you. Even though I appear before you today with sweaty palms, perhaps a slight tremor in my discourse, I assure you there's no way I'd take a pool of spiders over this.

Today, we acquire the piece of paper that tells us we are intelligent enough to become professionals. A few of you already have your professions all figured out but for those of you who do not, let me break it to you. You are about to embark on the most exciting yet incredibly stressful journey to date. I'm talking about getting a job. But if there's something I've learned from securing eight internships throughout my college career, which by the way has established me as one of the finest coffee makers and toilet seat sanitizers in all of Los Angeles, this is it: There is always going to be someone smarter than you, someone with more knowledge, with better work experience, with a more prestigious educational background.

Three months ago, I applied for a job at Fox Sports in the Music Licensing department. I didn't know much about the business, didn't know anyone in the business and I definitely didn't know anything about licensing. I knew it was a long shot and that hundreds of candidates were better qualified.

Long story short, I got the job. I beat out every single candidate that I went up against. And who am I? I'm no better or more deserving than anyone here. But I embraced the mentality that regardless of other factors, there is not a SINGLE person on this planet that will work harder than me, that will be a better all-around asset to the workplace, that will have my passion. It wasn't until I adopted this mentality that things finally started looking clearer for me.

Graduates; realize that there is NOBODY out there that will outwork you, that there is not a single person that will have your passion, your determination, your cojones. If you take on this mentality and use everything you learned at Cal Poly, there is absolutely nothing that can stop you.

I want to dedicate this award to my mother who taught me there is no such thing as impossible—rather, it is an excuse for those not willing to put in the extra effort. To my father, for teaching me that this diploma, those paychecks, and the professional accomplishments we will surmount do not signify success, it's the number of lives we better and our impact on humanity that will determine true achievement. I also want to dedicate this moment to my second mother and the most loving woman I have ever known, Marie Rupay, whom I know is proudly watching from the heavens with a big smile on her face.

Graduates; don't be the person that is always complaining about their job, about their boss, about not having enough pay. Be the person about whom your coworkers have nothing but great things to say, who manages their responsibilities with passion and care and strives to become an expert at everything he or she does, even if it's just answering phones or maintaining a schedule. Be the person who leaves this graduation ceremony today and goes on to become something so great that twenty years from now, high school students throughout the world will want to come to this university because today, right here and now, one of the most successful and influential individuals graduated from here. Be THAT person.

And the next time fear comes knocking on your door, don't cower. You open that door, look fear directly in the eye, and say, "get the hell off my property."

And, off fear went, off my property and back down the street. Sure, fear still comes around once in a while, but he only makes it halfway up the sidewalk before I catch him. Sometimes, I even let him in the front door— but on my terms. Truth is, fear is actually becoming a friend of mine. Pretty cool guy, once you get to know him.

CHAPTER 28:

A Final Message

"A book may give you excellent suggestions on how best to conduct yourself in the water, but sooner or later you must get wet, perhaps even strangle and be 'half scared to death.' There are a great many 'wet less' bathing suits worn at the seashore, but no one ever learns to swim in them. To plunge is the only way."

— DALE CARNEGIE

Writing a book is hard work. I've missed many outings, family get-togethers, and my daughter's birth because of this. Just kidding about that last one, but the rest is true.

What made writing this book so difficult wasn't a lack of passion, neither was it a lack of content. It was the fact that, for whatever reason, I was afraid of getting it all wrong. I figured...*Roy...most people die without ever writing a book. This is an incredible opportunity, it best be perfect!*

I know, I should have just written whatever came to mind and dealt with the details later. Instead, I pondered, second guessed and, often, found myself after spending five hours a day with only a half-page of work to show, trying to figure out what part of my mental development was to blame for my inability to write freely. As a result of my persistent struggles, I took a break from writing for four months to study the craft of writing.

I wanted to learn how to formulate stories, put ideas to paper, pace myself, and avoid writer's block. After a few months of study, I was set. I spent a couple of days putting together a strict schedule to follow. With that, I had an arsenal of newly acquired knowledge and an action plan to face any issue that might come my way.

I was absurdly inspired. Sometimes I felt so pumped that I'd whisper motivational stuff to myself in the mirror while making muffled-crowd-cheering noises. I'd imagine myself finishing a speech and tough guys tearing up as they applauded, famous orators doing the slow clap, and all the people I've let down standing there with tears in their eyes, mouthing, "You did it." This time, I was so ready....

Ready to start figuring out my writing style, that is! It didn't matter that I had already developed my own style from twenty years of writing—I just felt the need to keep searching for that "perfect" voice. "You must have an artillery of hand-picked weapons before going to war!" a writer wearing a fedora I met outside of a used bookstore in Silverlake once advised me. "Wow, that's a great metaphor! This guy is the real deal!" I thought.

As a result of that chance meeting, I started skimming through the public speaking books I had read and re-read throughout my school years. I took advice in bits and pieces from each, then started sending writing samples to a few of my old English professors to steer me in the right direction. When I got the feedback, I knew I was ready.

Ready, that is, to cross off all the items on my, "Seven Things You Must Know Before Writing a Non-Fiction Book" checklist!

1. *Why would someone want to read your book?*

Because they're getting tired of nearly having a nervous breakdown every time they have to give a speech and want to hear how to stop nearly having nervous breakdowns from someone who had a nervous breakdown for the same reason.

2. *Who wants to read your book?*

My parents and some of the people I helped with their public speaking issues. *I realize I've been doing a poor job of marketing my book (maybe I should postpone starting until I get an audience? Something to ponder).*

3. *Do you have enough content to fill a book?*

I definitely have enough content floating around in my brain to fill a book. Whether I'll finish before being paralyzed by carpal tunnel and/or radiation poisoning due to computer screen exposure, is another issue.

4. *How would you describe your book's contents?*

Passion-filled. Sometimes when I think of something awesome or inspirational to include in my book, I get strangely emotional. Once, as I was driving in bumper-to-bumper traffic on my way to work, an older woman in the car next to me noticed me drenched in tears and gestured to me to roll my window down. Sitting in 5 mph traffic, we went back and forth, me saying, "Really, I'm okay. They're happy tears," and her insisting I take down her number if I ever thought of doing something bad to myself.

5. *Why are you the best person to write this book?*

I overcame my horrific fear of public speaking and I know exactly what is needed to overcome this fear. I have the power of hindsight and a mile-long scroll of things I know now that I wish I had known when I was suffering with glossophobia.

6. *Is this the only book you'll write on this subject?*

Maybe when my career as a public speaker kicks off, I'll write a sequel called *Scared Speechless Episode 2* and make it *Star Wars* themed.

7. *How do you want to publish your book?*

I'll set up meetings with five big publishers. Prior to starting the meetings, I'll wink and sneak $100 into their butt pockets.

I survived the "Seven Things You Need to Know Before You Write Your Non-Fiction Book" test! Let's do this! I had all the information, I was motivated, and I was ready for anything.

But I didn't start. And this time, I couldn't make up an excuse. I had taken a four-month break from writing to prepare myself to do what I had already done: start writing. Though I wouldn't admit it at the time, I was afraid of getting started because I was afraid of not having an excuse if anything were to go wrong. I was scared that if I started my book and stopped twenty pages in, I would be deemed a failure—by me.

Nevertheless, just as I did with the fear of public speaking; I eventually got my thoughts in order, built an action plan, and achieved my goal of publishing this, my book.

I was told about halfway through this writing journey that if it had crossed my mind that this book would be my ticket to stardom, that I'd finally be able to pay for the kitchen remodel my parents have been dreaming of, or buy the new car I've been in desperate need of, I'd better brace myself for a rude awakening.

I'm fine with that. I wasn't at first; I secretly hoped I'd be deemed the next Dale Carnegie off the bat. If nothing else, I may garner a sliver of immortality with this book. Something nice to pull out of the old memory box and show to my grandkids when they're old enough to care. Isn't that what we're all after anyways?

But even if all evidence that this book ever existed is destroyed—say, in a public burning, due to my criminally hilarious sense of humor—and even if my grandkids can't look up from their digital screens long enough for me to say, "Look here children, your stinky ol' gramps wrote this book when he was a young chap," and this project earns me nothing more than a shiny nickel to throw in a fountain so I can wish for more nickels, I pray that I'm able to accomplish just one thing: help someone.

I'm clueless as to where I would be if I could have gotten over this fear earlier, say, in middle school. Maybe a Harvard graduate rising through the ranks at some top-notch investment firm? Perhaps I would have achieved my first dream of being a roller coaster designer? Who knows—what's gone is gone. Right now, I'm just hoping that my story will help someone overcome their fear. To you who are raring to bust out of fear's grip by reading this book, I trust I've provided sufficient inspiration that you'll keep fighting until you've realized your goal.

If this book did help you, I'd love it if you'd help me get the word out so it can help more people. Leave me an Amazon review, post about it on your social media sites, tell your schoolmates about it, gift it to a coworker, employ it as part of your fail-proof pick-up strategy for when you see someone sexy at the bar, or read it with a sensual tone to your husband (or wife) as a one hundred percent all-natural aphrodisiac. Totally kidding (maybe), but I'm hoping this will help enough people to start a nice buzz.

More importantly, shoot me an email and let me know how everything is going with you. I'd love to hear how you've progressed after reading this book and what I can do to help: royscaredspeechless@gmail.com

Until then, thanks for reading. And now that you have all the tools to unleash your inner badass speaker, get out there and wow 'em!

Works Cited and Research

Barry, Dave. *Dave Barry's Guide to Life*. New York: Wings, 1998. Print.

Bauby, Jean-Dominique. *The Diving Bell and the Butterfly*. New York: Random House, 1997. Print.

Brooks, Alison Wood. "Get Excited: Reappraising Pre-Performance Anxiety as Excitement." *Journal of Experimental Psychology: General* 143.3 (2014): 144-158. Web. 16 Sept. 2015. Digital.

Carnegie, Dale. *How to Develop Self-Confidence & Influence People by Public Speaking*. New York: Gallery Books, 2017. Print.

Carnegie, Dale. *The Quick and Easy Way to Effective Speaking*. New York: Pocket Books, 1962. Print.

De Cervantes, Miguel Saavedra. *Don Quixote*. Translated by Edith Grossman, Harper Perennial, 2005. Print.

DeGeneres, Ellen. *Introducing DJ Khaled*. YouTube. 9 March 2016. Web. 14 April 2017. Digital.

Dr. Suess. *Hooray for Diffendoofer Day*. New York: Knopf Books for Young Readers, 1998. Print.

Ford, Debbie. *The Best Year of Your Life: Dream It, Plan It, Live It*. New York: HarperCollins, 2006. Print.

Gladwell, Malcolm. *David and Goliath: Underdogs, Misfits, and the Art of Battling Giants*. New York: Little, Brown & Company, 2013. Print.

Gladwell, Malcolm. *Outliers: The Story of Success*. New York: Little, Brown & Company, 2008. Print.

Tracy, Brian. *Speak to Win: How to Present with Power in Any Situation.* New York: AMACOM, 2008. Print.

Godin, Seth. *Worst One Ever.* Web blog post. Seth's Blog. 9 June 2013. Web. 10 Oct. 2015. Digital.

Grout, Pam. *E-Squared: Nine Do-It-Yourself Energy Experiments That Prove Your Thoughts Create Your Reality.* Carlsbad: Hay House, 2013. Print.

Ingersoll, Robert G. *The Works of Robert G. Ingersoll: Tributes and Miscellany.* Vol. 12, Kessinger Publishing, LLC, 2010. Print.

Jamieson, Jeremy P., Wendy Berry Mendes, and Matthew Nock. "Public Speaking and Stress Responses." *Psychology Today*, 5 June 2013. Web. 09 Aug. 2015. Digital.

King, Stephen. *On Writing: A Memoir of the Craft.* New York: Pocket Books, 2000. Print.

Naftulin, Donald H., John E. Ware, and Frank A. Donnelly. "The Doctor Fox Lecture: A Paradigm of Educational Seduction." *Journal of Medical Education* 48, July 1973: 630-635. Digital.

Noonan, Peggy. *On Speaking Well: How to Give a Speech with Style, Substance, and Clarity.* New York: Regan Books, 1998. Print.

Scheier, Michael F. and Charles S. Carver. "Optimism, Coping, and Health: Assessment and Implications of Generalized Outcome Expectancies." *Health Psychology 4.3 (1985): 219-47. Web. 11 Sept. 2015. Digital.*

Sutherland, Kenneth. *Muddy Waters – Got My Mojo Workin.'* YouTube. 11 January 2007. Web. 29 August 2017. Video.

The Wolf of Wall Street. Directed by Martin Scorsese. Paramount Pictures, 2014. Film.

Tracy, Brian. *Speak to Win: How to Present with Power in Any Situation.* New York: AMACOM, 2008. Print.

Wallechinsky, David, and Amy Wallace. *The Book of Lists.* Canongate Books, 2005. Print.

Wheeler, Elmer. *How I Mastered My Fear of Public Speaking,* New York: Harper, 1957. Print.

We're the Millers. Directed by Rawson Marshall Thurber. Performers Jason Sudeikis and Jennifer Aniston. New Line Cinema, 2013. Film.

For a list of quotations from the following authors, please google "The Author's Name" and "Quotations": Sudha Chandran, Tina Fey, Sir Ralph Richardson, Theodore Roosevelt, Molly Weis.

Recommended Books

Note: The following is a list of references that either influenced my thoughts, my style, or just contributed to this wacky ride in some way, shape, or form. I highly recommend them all.

Brain Rules: 12 Principles for Surviving and Thriving at Work, Home, and School (Pear Press) – by John Medina

Don Quixote (Penguin Classics) – by Miguel de Cervantes, Edited/Translated by John Rutherford

Linchpin: Are You Indispensable? (Penguin Group) – by Seth Godin

My Life and Hard Times (Harper Perennial Modern Classics) – by James Thurber

Slide:ology: The Art and Science of Creating Great Presentations (O'Reilly) – by Nancy Duarte

The Disaster Artist (Simon & Schuster) – by Greg Sestero

Um: Slips, Stumbles, and Verbal Blunders, and What They Mean (Anchor) – by Michael Erard

You Are a Badass: How to Stop Doubting Your Greatness and Start Living an Awesome Life (Hachette Book Group) – by Jen Sincero

Made in the USA
San Bernardino,
CA

57194785R00183